LIFE'S LESSONS FROM LIFE'S LOSERS

Blessings,
Pastor Steve Dighton

Steve Dighton

Proverbs 3:5,6

WestBow Press books may be ordered through booksellers or by contacting:

WestBow Press
A Division of Thomas Nelson
1663 Liberty Drive
Bloomington, IN 47403
www.westbowpress.com
1-(866) 928-1240

ISBN: 978-1-4497-3396-4 (sc)

Library of Congress Control Number: 2011962386

Printed in the United States of America

WestBow Press rev. date: 1/16/2012

To Dr. Mary Dighton
my beautiful bride

Contents

Preface

Everyone who has ever competed in any arena of competition has suffered loss. It's unavoidable; it's the common denominator of all of humanity. While we like to think of ourselves as winners the truth is few of us win and none of us win all the time. But everyone knows the disappointment and the heartache of losing. We see the painful effects of losing on the face of an athlete who gets beat by a last second shot, or a game ending field goal or a sprint to the finish line. It happens in politics as after a season of a hard fought campaign the vote is counted and the results reveal what has been dreaded. But nevertheless the loser lives on. The challenge for all of us is what will we do with our defeat? Will we fall forward or will we allow defeat to be our destruction?

A few months ago, after 20 years of service, my church awarded me with a sabbatical. While this afforded me the opportunity to spend some uninterrupted time in God's Word it became strikingly obvious to me of how many personalities in the Word of God could fit under the banner of losers. So I prayerfully considered the twelve who made my final cut, but believe me the list is far from exhaustive. The pages of God's Word are saturated with people who destroyed their lives through disobedience and pride.

The great truth of the gospel is that Jesus Christ came to deliver us from the failure of sin and the finality of death. It is only through Him that losers are made winners through believing faith in Him.

Acknowledgments

There are several people that I want to acknowledge in making the writing and publishing of this book possible:

First, I want to thank my wife, Dr. Mary Dighton, who for 40+ years has been my best friend and completer. Mary has faithfully been by my side every Sunday morning; listening to me preach the same message twice and for many years three times a Sunday. She is my greatest encourager and I have relied on her praise and also her critique of my messages over the years. She happily took on this project spending countless hours researching various options, reformatting my manuscripts, looking up reverences for footnotes, and correcting my verb tenses. Without Mary, publishing this book could never have happened. She is an awesome wife and I thank her for being totally devoted to me and the ministry to which we have been called.

Second, I want to thank my Administrative Assistant, Kris Taylor. Kris helps me stay on top of my busy schedule, typed and organized the original manuscripts, and has been a dear friend and faithful church member for 21 years. Thank you for your constant help.

Thirdly, I want to thank the ministerial staff at Lenexa Baptist Church. All of these men make the ministry a real joy. We work together as a team; united, with a common goal to glorify God in all we do and to accomplish the mission to which we have been called. I give my sincere thanks to all of you.

Last but not least, I thank the deacons and the congregation of Lenexa Baptist Church. I am forever grateful to have the privilege to be your Pastor. I dare say there is no Pastor anywhere who feels more loved and supported by their church members. Thank you deacons and congregation for making Lenexa Baptist a “winning” church.

Chapter One

Raising Cain

Genesis 4:1–15

I. A FRACTURED FAMILY
   A. Their Offspring
   B. Their Occupations
   C. Their Offerings

II. A FORTELLING FACE
   A. Cain's Wrath
   B. God's Warning
   C. Cain's Wickedness

III. A FORSAKEN FUTURE
   A. The Condemnation
   B. The Commiseration
   C. The Configuration

The Word of God is overflowing with a multitude of people whose lives serve as positive examples for us to follow. In it we are equally flooded with a number of failures—people who made wrong decisions, poor choices—men who gave into temptations, who worshipped the Baal's, and who took the low road of compromise and ruin.

No doubt there are lessons to be learned from the many great examples of faith, obedience and Godliness, but conversely there is much to learn from the villains, the infidels, the deceitful and the deceivers—men we can only label as "losers". I'll be honest with you; I really dislike the term "loser". It is a derogatory tag that sounds condescending and brash. Still, the best way to define a loser is to say it's someone who failed. It's someone who didn't succeed, someone who missed their chance, someone who often times played the fool.

Here's what I know, most of life's lessons are learned not in our victories, but in our defeats; not in the best days, but in our darkest days. My prayer for you as you read this book and consider these twelve losers is that you will be determined to learn from their mistakes and be dedicated to being a winner in God's eyes. This is the very hope and promise of the gospel; that we can begin again in Jesus Christ, for in Him "old things have passed away; behold, all things have become new" (II Cor. 5:17, NKJV).

From the book of Genesis we will begin our evaluation of Life's Lessons from Life's Losers by considering Cain—the first born son of Adam and Eve who typifies and personifies the theme of this series.

I. A FRACTURED FAMILY

Adam was intimate with his wife Eve, and she conceived and gave birth to Cain. She said, "I have had a male child with the LORD'S help." Then she also gave birth to his brother Abel. Now Abel became a shepherd of flocks, but Cain worked the ground. In the course of time Cain presented some of the land's produce as an offering to the LORD. And Abel also presented an offering—some of the firstborn of his flock and their fat portions. The LORD had regard for Abel and his offering, (Gen. 4:1–4)

The preceding chapter of Genesis tells the story of the fall of man. God had told Adam and Eve that they could freely eat from any of the trees in the garden except for one—the tree of the knowledge of good and evil. You may be familiar with the story. The serpent tempts Eve and she eats of the forbidden fruit and also gives some to her husband, Adam. As a result of their disobedience they experienced the judgment of God. They had been cast out of the Garden of Eden. While they received the penalty for their sin, we also see that they received the grace of God. As He had promised, if they ate of the Tree of the Knowledge of Good and Evil, they would surely "die". While indeed that would be the ultimate reality, it was not an immediate reality. God sent them out of the Garden of Eden to work the ground and to be fruitful and multiply.

A. Their Offspring

Adam and Eve's firstborn son was named Cain. The Hebrew word is "qanah" which means acquired or brought forth. In essence, Adam and Eve had acquired a treasure from God, a baby, and Eve held this precious treasure in her arms. While she embraced him and gazed at his little face her head must have raced to the future with wonder at the thought of the joy that this new life would bring them and she surely marveled with anticipation of all that this tiny infant would grow up to be and do. Little did she know that she was holding the first murderer—and that the victim would be her second born son, Abel.

God's plan for the family is clearly seen here with the story of Adam and Eve—one man and one woman; a strong bond in a forever relationship. Yet, still the perversions and dysfunction of this first family unit was soon evident—it was a fractured family.

B. Their Occupations

We read that Cain was a farmer and Abel was a shepherd. According to Jewish tradition, Eve had a dream that revealed that Cain would do something harmful to Abel, so Adam had separated the boys, giving them different occupations. We read that Cain tilled the ground while Abel was a keeper of sheep.

C. Their Offerings

Both Cain and Abel knew about God and understood that He required offerings from them. As you might expect, Cain brought something from his livelihood as did Abel. However, Hebrews 11:4 clearly tells us "by faith Abel offered to God a better sacrifice than Cain did." The only conclusion to make is this—Cain offered a bloodless offering and while the produce from his harvest might have been the logical thing to give to God, it wasn't an offering that was approved by God. Later Levitical offerings of grain and fruit would be accepted by God, but the first offering would always be a sin offering.

I believe we see here in our text the first plank of the scriptural platform of truth—"without shedding of blood, there is no remission" (Heb. 9:22, NKJV). The Levitical law commanded it, but it had been modeled by God Himself as He took a sacrificial animal to make garments of skin to cover the sin and shame of Adam and Eve.

Abel, on the other hand, offered a sacrificial lamb and it was an acceptable sacrifice approved by God. Donald Grey Barnhouse writes: "The highway to the cross was now firmly established. Here the first lamb is seen, one lamb for one man. Later, at the Passover, there will be one lamb for one household (Exodus 12). Then, on the Day of Atonement, there will be one sacrifice for the nation (Leviticus 16). Finally, it is Christ who takes away the sin of the world" (John 1:29).[1] This was God's way of illustrating the awesome power of the bleeding Lamb. One Lamb saves a man, then a household, then a nation, and finally, through the Lamb of God, there is salvation for the whole world.

Don't miss the point of the story though. Although the offering of Cain was rejected, God didn't abandon Cain, but approached him to give him a warning, a truth that he must guard against—sin is at his door. We soon learn of the depravity and deviancy of Cain's heart. As Jeremiah declared, "the heart is deceitful above all things, and desperately wicked; who can know it?" (Jer. 17:9, NKJV).

This tragedy was more than sibling rivalry; something that seems to persist in many families where brothers and sisters compete with one another to win their parents' approval. We see sibling rivalry played out many times in the scriptures—with Jacob and Esau, Rachel and Leah, and especially with Joseph's brothers who are so jealous they sold him into slavery to get rid of him! But the original prototype for sibling rivalry was seen here in Cain and his disdainfulness for his brother Abel.

In the Greek language, there are four words for love—one of those is "phileo" which means brotherly love. It is synonymous with friendship love. It's a unique love that brothers should have for one another but when that phileo love is replaced by jealousy, envy, or retaliation, families become fractured. Actually, when Cain is mentioned in I John 3, the Apostle John is contrasting the personality of Cain with that of Jesus. Cain was void of love and murdered his brother. Jesus, being full of love, laid down His life for His brothers. Then in verse 15 John writes: "Everyone who hates his brother is a murderer, and you know that no murderer has eternal life residing in him."

II. A FORTELLING FACE

But he did not have regard for Cain and his offering. Cain was furious, and he looked despondent. Then the LORD said to Cain, "Why are you furious? And why do you look despondent? If you do what is right, won't you be accepted? But if you do not do what is right, sin is crouching at the door. Its desire is for you, but you must rule over it." Cain said to his brother Abel, "Let's go out to the field." And while they were in the field, Cain attacked his brother Abel and killed him. Then the LORD said to Cain, "Where is your brother Abel?" "I don't know," he replied. "Am I my brother's guardian?" (Gen. 4:5–9)

We read that the countenance on the face of Cain revealed his thoughts. The anger, bitterness and resentment that reside within the recesses of his heart are now being manifested outwardly. The internal is becoming the external.

Isaiah would later prophecy this truth. "The look on their faces testifies against them…They flaunt their sin. They do not conceal it. Woe to them" (Isa. 3:9). The great Roman philosopher and politician, Cicero, said: "All action is of the mind and the mirror of the mind is the face."[2]

A. Cain's Wrath

Cain was furious, enraged, with obvious misplaced anger. He couldn't get to God who didn't receive his offering so he turned his wrath on his brother Abel. His fury was relative to his jealousy. Rather than taking personal responsibility for his actions, he pointed a finger at Abel and was determined to pour out his wrath on him. Psalms 4:4 tells us, "Be angry and do not sin: on your bed, reflect in your heart and be still." That is exactly the admonition God is giving Cain. He is saying, "Cain, don't let the emotion of your feelings, the passion of your anger, lead you to act wrongly or irrationally. Think about this. Reflect on it before you take action." Let me assure you, any decision that's made when anger, revenge and hostility rule will always be regretted afterward. We need to cool down and think soberly. As my good friend, Pastor Derek Lynch likes to say, "When emotions are high, logic is low". Thus we don't want to respond in haste or else we will also go the way of Cain.

This type of instant retaliatory crime is sometimes called a crime of passion. I recently read that crimes of passion are referred to as Laws of Texas, since jurors there seem to be more lenient to those who've retaliated against their spouse or have even killed their spouse because they were caught cheating on them. In our text, Cain's fury was being stoked by the rod of revenge and his wrath was about to be his downfall.

B. God's Warning

God says, "Even though your sacrifice wasn't rightly given and offered in faith, still the offense of retaliation and vengeance can be avoided." Then He says, "Sin is crouching at the door. Its desire is for you, but you must master it" (Gen. 4:7). What a picture of how sin can overtake any of us. It's always crouching at the door of our lives, sometimes it crosses the threshold, moves into our house and soon it has us by the throat.

Consider this with me—In what ways do we find sin crouching at our door?

- It may be at work with a colleague of the opposite sex. Are things getting a bit too friendly? It seems harmless at first, but in your heart you are well aware that sin is making its way farther and farther into your house.

- It may be on the internet where sexual fantasy is only one click away. You convince yourself that this is not harming anyone else. It is just between you and your computer but you soon realize that your sexual resistance is in a downward spiral and you are soon looking for more than a heated up internet photo. Sin is getting a strangle hold on your neck.
- It may be a chance to fabricate an expense report or falsify personal income. You tell yourself you will make it right on the next report but the ease of the extra dollars is worth more than your integrity. Sin has moved in and is living comfortably in your home.
- It might be that you're just waiting to give someone a piece of your mind. You have convinced yourself that you are justified in this bit of irrational behavior. Sin has become your mentor and is teaching you the ways of destruction.
- Sin takes on the personification of lust, of greed, of lewdness, of dishonesty, of unfaithfulness, of flirtation. Believe me; it's always crouching at the door of our lives and is often disguised as a faithful friend, a confidant, a well deserved source of entertainment. We knowingly see through this disguise and yet we think that we can invite it in. We convince ourselves that we have the strength to master it.

How can we drive the demons of sin out and cleanse this old house in which we live? We cannot do it on our own. The Lord once told a story recorded in Matthew 12 of a man who once was possessed of a devil. The devil left him but later decided to return to his former house bringing seven other devils with him to take possession of it. Matthew records in verse 45: "As a result, that man's last condition is worse than the first." In essence, we are inadequate without God's help and His rule in our lives. Jesus tells us if we are going to master sin, we must first be mastered by Him who is able to master it.

Cain invited sin in. It became a comfortable relationship. It got a stranglehold around his neck and mastered him. God's warning was ignored.

C. Cain's Wickedness

As we read on in the text we see that we have the first murder. Cain rejected the wisdom of God which was spoken to him by God Himself. He rejected doing the right thing. He refused to repent and now in what seems to be a premeditated act, he invites Abel out to a killing field. Vengeance had won out. Sin had pounced on him and he turned from just being mad to being a murderer. Undoubtedly he invited Abel to the field because he thought it was there that he could get away with the crime. No one would ever need to know what happened. No one would ever witness what he was going to do. He could fabricate a story, blame it on a wild animal, deny he knew anything about it, and he would get away with it without a single soul knowing the truth. The first murderer also becomes the first liar. The hardness and the hatred of his heart are revealed in this cynical response as he says, "Look—I don't know what happened, but know this, I'm not responsible for the guy!"

I'm afraid masses of people today have gone the way of Cain with this attitude of indifference. "Hey, I'm not my brother's keeper. Don't bother me with your issues." Just like the lady in New York City who was recently murdered while thirty of her neighbors heard her cries but chose to do nothing. Jesus illustrated this indifferent attitude with the parable about the Good Samaritan. The Priest and the Levite walked on by the beaten man surely with this detached attitude—"Am I my brother's keeper?"

I detect some sarcasm coming from Cain's lips as he uttered this response to God. Abel had been the "keeper of sheep" and now was he was supposed to be the keeper of the one who was a keeper? Cain's indifference to God's warning resulted in the heinous murder of his own brother.

What is it about a person that designates them as a loser? I'll tell you. It's the person who misses out on the blessings of God because they neglect God's warning. It's someone who calls sin a friend. It's someone who lies and deceives. It's someone who hates and allows his hatred to ruin his life—which brings me to my final point.

III. A FORSAKEN FUTURE

Then He said, "What have you done? Your brother's blood cries out to Me from the ground! So now you are cursed with alienation from the ground that opened its mouth to receive your brother's blood you have shed. If you work the land, it will never again give you its yield. You will be a restless wanderer on the earth." But Cain answered the LORD, "My punishment is too great to bear! Since You are banishing me today from the soil, and I must hide myself from Your presence and become a restless wanderer on the earth, whoever finds me will kill me." Then the LORD replied to him, "In that case, whoever kills Cain will suffer vengeance seven times over." And He placed a mark on Cain so that whoever found him would not kill him. (Gen. 4:10–15)

Cain quickly realized his sins had found him out and God confronted him with the knowledge that what he had done had been done in God's sight. God made it known to Cain that what he had done was well known to Him because the blood of Abel cried out to Him. Abel was the first to visit the place the Bible calls Sheol (the place of death). He was the first person to die in faith. II Corinthians 5:8 is a comforting verse for the believer, "We are confident, yes, well pleased rather to be absent from the body and to be present with the Lord" (NKJV). While Abel's body lay slain in a field of hatred, Abel's spirit went to be with the Lord.

Hear me in this—everyone reading this has a future destination as well. We're all going to Sheol someday. Hebrews 9:27 says, "And just as it is appointed for people to die once—and after this, judgment". For each and every one of you who put your trust in Jesus, you have an eternal home in heaven—not made with human hands but with the nail scarred hands of our Savior. That's the promise of Jesus in John 14:3, "If I go away and prepare a place for you, I will come back and receive you to Myself, so that where I am you may be also." Everyone who rejects Jesus Christ is a loser. They have lost out on eternity. Oh, they may have known success in this world, but it will crumble to a cinder in the day of their judgment.

Let me remind you of Jesus warning question, "For what will it profit a man if he gains the whole world, and loses his own soul?" (Mark 8:36, NKJV). Consider for yourself this pointed question from our Savior before we look at three concluding truths from our text.

A. The Condemnation

The curse pronounced from God was relative to the livelihood of Cain. It concerned the productivity of the soil. To a farmer like Cain, this was severe. It means Cain could not expect to establish roots in one place—always having to till new ground. He would have to be a vagabond, a wanderer, and a fugitive in this world. Still today, one of the most despised people in all central and Eastern Europe are the gypsies (The Romani people). They're called strangers in a strange land. They are looked upon with suspicion. They are targets of hostile laws and in many countries they are forbidden to buy land. They are often the scapegoats and the disenfranchised. Cain led the way in becoming this people of shame.

B. The Commiseration

Cain quickly exclaimed that this punishment was more than he could bear. He couldn't stand the thought of being a vagabond and a fugitive. He was fearful for his own life after having complete disregard for the life of his own brother.

God did not establish the death penalty for a person who took the life of another until He made his covenant with Noah. Actually, there are eighteen crimes in the Old Testament that mandate capital punishment but Cain would escape that coming divine decree. His life would be lived out in guilt and shame, proving the truth of the writer of Proverbs, "the way of the transgressor is hard" (Prov. 13:15, KJV).

C. The Configuration

Cain cried out for mercy and God gave him protection and promised a seven-fold vengeance for anyone who harmed him. The Lord put a mark on him. We can only speculate what this identifiable mark was, but while this unique configuration saved him from personal harm, it undoubtedly marked the shame of his offense.

Let's recount the life lessons we can learn from Cain.

1. **We're required to give what God desires and deserves, not merely what we prefer.**

Abel's offering was acceptable. It was a sacrificial lamb. While Cain brought an offering, it was unacceptable to God. It was not what God required. To reiterate again, there is no remission of sin without the shedding of blood. Today the only way you can come to Christ is through the blood bought salvation purchased at Calvary. The best you can give is as filthy rags. "Repent ye therefore, and be converted, that your sins may be blotted out" (Acts 3:19, KJV).

2. **Bitterness, jealousy, and hatred will cause you despair and alienation.**

Cain's anger toward God and his brother resulted in a life of loneliness and fear as he wandered aimlessly the rest of his life. Be assured that if you allow bitterness, jealousy and hatred to reside within your heart; you too will find yourself alone and isolated.

3. **Real repentance is evidenced in Godly sorrow, not simply in grievous remorse.**

Cain hated that he was exiled from the presence of God, yet he never called out to God in repentance and forgiveness. Here is what I know without a doubt….loser's can become winners if they come home to God. Don't go the way of Cain but let your remorse lead you to true repentance.

Chapter Two

The Biggest Loser

Matthew 26:14–15

I. A PRETENTIOUS PERPETRATOR
- A. His Position
- B. His Prophecies
- C. His Payment

II. A PREDETERMINED PLOT
- A. The Prediction
- B. The Perplexity
- C. The Person
- D. The Place

III. A PREDICTABLE PLIGHT
- A. His Remorse
- B. His Remains

One of the most popular prime time television shows is on NBC and is entitled "The Biggest Loser". If you haven't seen it, it is a competition where extremely overweight people, both men and women, lose all dignity and shame and seek to lose more weight than the competition. As of the writing of this book I think the record is 264 pounds. The objective and the goal of the show are to become the Biggest Loser. I can't think of any other competition where that is the quest—to lose!

As we look at our Biggest Loser we are not looking at his weight loss or even looking for merely some interesting entertainment. Like watching the television show we are seeking to learn some positive truths from a negative example that will motivate us to avoid even being in the competition for the title of The Biggest Loser. Surely if there is one person who comes to mind as a loser, it is Judas. He is undoubtedly the most devilish, despised and devious character who ever lived. That is why I am bestowing on him the title of The Biggest Loser. Anytime we deny, betray, or sell-out our Savior we, not unlike Judas, become a loser as well. I am afraid, though, that there is a little Judas in all of us. We play the hypocrite. We impersonate the authentic. We say one thing with our lips and yet live a contradictory life.

When you read the gospel accounts of Jesus instituting the sacred ordinance of communion we find the gospel writers mention Judas in every account. His story is the tragic story of what can happen when sin, selfishness and greed make their way into our hearts. Judas is a case-in-point of what can happen to anyone who makes a decision in haste without considering the implications. As I often say—"we're all just one step away from stupid!" Certainly, while the results of our choices may not be as notable as Judas', still they can wreck our life and take us down to the depths of despair.

I. A PRETENTIOUS PERPETRATOR

Then one of the Twelve—the man called Judas Iscariot—went to the chief priests and said, "What are you willing to give me if I hand Him over to you?" So they weighed out 30 pieces of silver for him. (Matthew 26:14–15)

As you study the biblical account of the disciples, you learn of the divine call of Peter, Andrew, James, John and Matthew—but not so with Judas. In the gospels he is simply referred to as one of the twelve. However, it is noteworthy that in Scripture Judas never referred to Jesus as more than "Rabboni" meaning teacher. He never accepted Him as his personal Savior and Lord. Possibly, he was just caught up in the charisma of Jesus and he expected that Jesus was going to establish an earthly kingdom. He wanted to be involved in that but when he saw that his errant idea was crumbling all he wanted to do was to get what he could salvage, and he soon would "sell out the Son of God." He forever became known as the Galilean betrayer.

Judas was pretentious. He identified with the disciples. He was just as near to the Savior's redeeming touch as they but his heart was cold and indifferent. Jesus said of his kind, "These people honor Me with their lips, but their heart is far from Me" (Matt. 15:8). I want you to notice three things about Judas.

A. His Position

Judas was the treasurer, the money keeper for the ministry of Jesus as they traveled the Galilean countryside. In John 12 we learn about his position as the keeper of the moneybox. While the operating funds were no doubt meager, still it was necessary to have someone in charge of the funds, and that responsibility fell to Judas. Why this is we can only speculate. Maybe he was believed to be the most trustworthy or maybe he appeared to be the most frugal, but at any rate he shouldered the responsibility of balancing the books and keeping the meager assets of this itinerant ministry. Perhaps it was simply a part of God's master plan because it was Judas' greed and his love of money and the power that accompanies it that set the entire betrayal plot in motion. Remember what Solomon declared in Ecclesiastes 5:10, "The one who loves money is never satisfied with money, and whoever loves wealth is never satisfied with income. This too is futile." The blood money that Judas received not only didn't satisfy it also repulsed him.

B. His Prophecies

While we are introduced to Judas in the New Testament as one of the twelve, we actually read several Old Testament prophecies that spoke plainly and prophetically of him, for he was the one that was coming as the betrayer.

- Zechariah 11 speaks of the thirty pieces of silver that Judas would receive to betray the Savior.

- In Psalms 109:8 the death of Judas is prophesied and his replacement is mentioned in what would transpire in Acts 1.
- Psalm 41:9 says, "Even my friend in whom I trusted, one who ate my bread, has lifted up his heel against me."

According to Arthur Pierson in his book, Many Infallible Proofs, there are 332 Old Testament prophecies that are fulfilled in the life and ministry of Jesus.[3] While we read prophecies about Jesus' birth, His behavior, His benevolence, His bravery, we learn also about His betrayer—Judas would be the son of perdition.

C. His Payment

Judas approached the chief priests at the house of Caiaphas. Judas knew they had been lying in wait for the Savior so he asked them, "How much is Jesus worth to you?" In other words, if I pull a "Benedict Arnold" and turn traitor and entrap him, what's it worth? They declared "30 pieces of silver", which according to the Torah is the price of a slave.

Some of you are now thinking, "Wow, I can't believe Judas sold Jesus out for 30 pieces of silver." Quite honestly, I know many people who have sold Him out for a lot less than that. You see, every time you let bitterness and a lack of forgiveness have its way with you, every time your behavior misrepresents your belief, you sell Jesus out. People sell Jesus out at the casino, at a football game, at the office. It doesn't even require 30 pieces of silver. When we sell Jesus out, we prove there is a little Judas in all of us.

II. A PREDETERMINED PLOT

And from that time he started looking for a good opportunity to betray Him…..So the disciples did as Jesus had directed them and prepared the Passover. When evening came, He was reclining at the table with the Twelve. While they were eating, He said, "I assure you: One of you will betray Me." Deeply distressed, each one began to say to Him, "Surely not I, Lord?" He replied, "The one who dipped his hand with Me in the bowl—he will betray Me. The Son of Man will go just as it is written about Him, but woe to that man by whom the Son of Man is betrayed! It would have been better for that man if he had not been born." Then Judas, His betrayer, replied, "Surely not I, Rabbi?" (Matthew 26:16, 19–25)

We read in Chapter 12 of John's gospel that while visiting at the house of Lazarus Judas becomes incensed that Mary used some costly perfume to anoint Jesus. Judas piously declared, "That oil was costly. It could have been sold and the money given to the poor." John wrote a one verse commentary on Judas. "He didn't say this because he cared about the poor but because he was a thief. He was in charge of the money-bag and would steal part of what was put in it" (John 12:6). We also read, "Before the Passover Festival, Jesus knew that His hour had come to depart from this world to the Father. Having loved His own who were in the world, He loved them to the end. Now by the time of supper, the Devil had already put it into the heart of Judas, Simon Iscariot's son, to betray Him" (John 12:1–2).

We read in two of the gospel accounts that Satan entered Judas. The question becomes, was Judas nothing but a pawn in the hand of Satan or was he acting on his own free will? Was he predestined to betray the Son of God or was he simply doing what his wicked heart desired? The answer to both is yes. Judas could have chosen against this insidious plot to crucify Jesus, but his greedy and wicked heart wouldn't let him. Could Judas have disrupted the mission and the master plan of redemption or was he merely predestined to be the fall guy? You see, he could have, but he couldn't have. It's the age old argument of predestination vs. free will. It's truly one of the paradoxes of the Scriptures—God predestines things and then gives men the free will to chose, and never do the two conflict. Judas could have chosen to disrupt the plot, but something in his own heart wouldn't let him. In his vulnerable and unregenerate state, Satan came and entered him and the determined and destructive plot was soon to be executed. While Judas could have refused his place in the crucifixion plot, he could not have refused his place. Understand this, God's sovereign will and man's free will are both taught in the

Scriptures. When two truths that seems to contradict each other are both true, it's called an antinomy. Webster's dictionary defines it as, "A contradiction between two apparently equally valid principles or between inferences correctly drawn from such principles."[4] In other words, its two principles that stand side-by-side that are seemingly irreconcilable, yet both are undeniable. So it is with predestination and human responsibility.

While Judas was the appointed son of perdition, it did not dismiss or excuse his devious, devilish betrayal, for nowhere in the Scriptures does prophecy or predestination cancel human responsibility—not in Judas' life and not in your life.

Now in the text I notice first….

A. The Prediction

The disciples are reclining at the table, eating the Passover meal together in the Upper Room. In the ancient Near East, eating a meal with someone was a mark of friendship, thus compounding the treachery. Jesus unveils the news that there is a betrayer among them. This was certainly not the first time he had brought up that disparaging deed. All the way back in chapter 6 of John's gospel we read that many of His followers abandoned Jesus to follow Him no more. He said, "Didn't I choose you, The Twelve? Yet one of you is the Devil!" (John 6:70). It seems the reality of that prediction had not yet been comprehended and this is the first use of the word "betrayer". The word means "to give over" and is used of delivering a prisoner over to a person for punishment.

B. The Perplexity

Surely, not I Lord was the cry and question from each of the disciples. It seems they were all rightfully concerned that it could possibly be them. They each had certainly received the rebuke of Jesus before and now they were being brought face to face with the sinfulness of their own hearts. Jesus' response in verse 23 did nothing to alleviate their anxiety because undoubtedly each of them had dipped his hand in the bowl. But in John's Upper Room discourse we read, "I'm not speaking about all of you; I know those I have chosen. But the Scripture must be fulfilled: The one who eats My bread has raised his heel against Me" (John 13:18). Jesus quotes from Psalm 41:9 where David was betrayed by Ahithophel, as he sided up with Absalom in his coup against David. Jesus concludes by saying, in essence, this is the mission for which I came, but woe to the betrayer. He's the big loser and it would have been better for him not to ever have been born!

C. The Person

Judas is responding with the others, but in order to not say anything that might have incriminated him, he calls Jesus "Teacher." Jesus didn't respond with a direct accusation but simply declared to him, you have said it yourself. You're guilty and you'll be responsible for your actions.

Judas had fixed his place as the arch sinner of all human history. He had allowed his carnal and unregenerate heart to take him to the place of no return and Jesus said, "What you're doing, do quickly" (John 13:27).

D. The Place

We read after the Last Supper concluded that they sang a hymn went out into the night and came to a place—a garden called Gethsemane which means "oil press". It was a place where Jesus and His disciples frequently went. I have been there many times in my visits to Israel. It's just across the Kidron Valley from Jerusalem where ancient olive trees, some 2000 years old, still stand today.

Judas was well acquainted with Jesus' habits and knew that He had been to the garden many times to pray. He knew he would find Him in Gethsemane. Sure enough—Judas showed up and gave the betrayal kiss to the Savior. Jesus was apprehended and taken to the House of Caiaphas where the mock trial which led to the crucifixion was now set in motion.

III. A PREDICTABLE PLIGHT

Then Judas, His betrayer, seeing that He had been condemned, was full of remorse and returned the 30 pieces of silver to the chief priests and elders. "I have sinned by betraying innocent blood," he said. "What's that to us?" they said. "See to it yourself!" So he threw the silver into the sanctuary and departed. Then he went and hanged himself. (Matthew 27:3–5)

As we close the story on this "biggest loser" we see where his betrayal took him. What a pitiful and predictable conclusion to one who had been so close to the Savior.

A. His Remorse

It seems now, even to Judas, that his betrayal had become disdainful and despicable. He threw the blood money into the Temple, went out and hung himself—the predictable plight for anyone who commits such a grievous sin.

The age old question we ask is this; was Judas repentant? I submit to you that he was regretful but that he was not repentant. Remorse and regret are not synonymous with repentance. I've known many people who were regretful, even remorseful for their behavior but not repentant. Remember, repentance is evidenced by doing "an about face." Judas was regretful and remorseful but it led to his suicide, not a turning to God. Paul would later write, "For godly sorrow produces repentance leading to salvation, not to be regretted; but the sorrow of the world produces death" (II Cor. 7:10, NKJV). Worldly sorrow is what Judas had. It always leads to death. I want to ask you—have you ever really repented of your sins? ".... but unless you repent, you will all perish as well!" (Luke 13:3). Sometimes, in our lives, our response is regret because we got caught. There is so much shame and embarrassment associated with our sin that we are full of regret. But true repentance brings us back to God. We see the example of this in the story of the prodigal son—he came to himself, meaning he repented, turned from his sin, did an about face, which sent him straight back to the Father.

Judas tried to undo his evil plot by returning the money, but it was too late. The wheels of God's sovereign plan were in motion and Judas' life ended in despair without ever being reconciled to the Lord Jesus. Sinner friend, I beg you today, don't lose out on so great a salvation. Today is the day of salvation. Now is the accepted time.

B. His Remains

Speaking of Judas in the book of Acts we read, "Now this man acquired a field with his unrighteous wages; and falling headfirst, he burst open in the middle, and all his insides spilled out. This became known to all the residents of Jerusalem, so that in their own language that field is called Hakeldama, that is, Field of Blood" (Acts 1:18–19). It seems the blood money was used to purchase a tract of land in the Valley of Hinnom called Aramarc Akel Dama—Field of Blood or Potter's Field. Luke, the writer of Acts, says here that Judas fell headlong and his entrails gushed out. Don't confuse his falling headlong with hanging himself. It seems that either a branch on the tree on which he hung himself or what he hung himself with gave way. In a grotesque and graphic description, we see the remains of one who lost out and paid the consequences.

Here, I ask the question—is there a little Judas in you today? If so, repent of it and return to the Savior, lest you become life's loser.

Chapter Three

Your Achan Heart Will Tell On You

Joshua 7

I. A HEART OF COVETOUSNESS

II. A HATRED OF COMPROMISE

III. A HARVEST OF CONSEQUENCES

A. Dishonored God
B. Defeat to God's People
C. Disgraced His Parents
D. Death to His Children

We are going to look at the book of Joshua in the Old Testament. God's people now had crossed the Jordan and entered into the land of promise. The wilderness wanderings were over. Moses had passed the mantle of leadership to Joshua and things were finally looking up. Forty nomadic years of aimless wanderings were now being swallowed up in victory.

Chapter six is about the victory at Jericho, the infamous walled city where God miraculously took down the walls and handed that Canaanite city over to Joshua and his people. But what happens next is startling and it was relative to capturing a small insignificant city called Ai—so diminutive that only a couple of thousand troops would be needed to conquer it. But the unthinkable took place, the men of Ai struck down several of the Israelite men, chased them out of the city and as a result the people's hearts melted in discouragement. What in the world happened? Something went terribly wrong. We're going to see that not only some**thing** went wrong, but some**one** was responsible. The defeat lay at the feet of one man.

I have a question for you. Did you ever know anyone who pulled defeat from the jaws of victory? I can't help but think of Leon Lett, former defensive lineman for the Dallas Cowboys, who also went to Emporia State University, (for all of you who are from Kansas). Remember that snowy Thanksgiving Day in 1993 when, in the closing seconds of the game between Miami and Dallas, Leon tried to recover a blocked field goal that Miami was kicking to win the game? If Leon didn't do anything, the Cowboys win 14–13. But instead, he muffed the recovery; Miami got the ball and won the game with no time left. As you know, that wasn't Leon's only blunder…lest you forget the Super Bowl 1994 against Buffalo. Leon was able to pull defeat from the jaws of victory again.

Something not unlike that happened with a man named Achan here in our text. God's conquest of Canaan was in motion. Victory that had been longed for, for decades had been experienced at Jericho. But suddenly there was a surprising and paralyzing defeat. We are going to learn a life lesson from a loser named Achan and we discover "Your Achan Heart Will Tell on you".

I. A HEART OF COVETOUSNESS

The Israelites, however, were unfaithful regarding the things set apart for destruction. Achan son of Carmi, son of Zabdi, son of Zerah, of the tribe of Judah, took some of what was set apart, and the LORD's anger burned against the Israelites. Joshua sent men from Jericho to Ai, which is near Beth-aven, east of Bethel, and told them, "Go up and scout the land." So the men went up and scouted Ai. After returning to Joshua they reported to him, "Don't send all the people, but send about 2,000 or 3,000 men to attack Ai. Since the people of Ai are so few, don't wear out all our people there." So about 3,000 men went up there, but they fled from the men of Ai. The men of Ai struck down about 36 of them and chased them from outside the gate to the quarries, striking them down on the descent. As a result, the people's hearts melted and became like water. (Joshua 7:1–5)

We are going to look at three things in this captivating narrative. Achan, we learn, was from the tribe of Judah—the elite tribe that would be the renowned tribe of our Savior, as Jesus was the lion of Judah. We quickly learn in this narrative the personal and even the national effects that one man's sin can have. Achan, because of a heart of covetousness, not only brought destruction to himself and his immediate family, but his disobedience cost the entire nation of Israel their first defeat in the Promised Land.

In Joshua chapter six, we read about the incredible victory at Jericho. This is the victory where God overpowered the walled Canaanite citadel simply by His people following His command to encircle the city. Then when Joshua gave the command, the priests blew the trumpets, the people shouted and the walls were demolished and desecrated. God also gave some very specific instructions about the spoils in Jericho. "But keep yourselves from the things set apart, or you will be set apart for destruction. If you take any of those things, you will set apart the camp of Israel for destruction and bring disaster on it. For all the silver and gold, and the articles of bronze and iron, are dedicated to the Lord and must go into the Lord's treasury" (Joshua 6:18–19). The temptation of the silver, gold and beautiful garments was too great a temptation for Achan and soon his "Achan heart" would tell on him. Be assured of this….greed has the potential and power to take any man down. Boyd Bailey writes: "Money-motivated people are never content and it leads one to compromise character and common sense."[5] Achan's flawed character and his lack of conviction would soon be evident. I can see Achan lying in his tent thinking about all the value of the precious things that were left unprotected only a few hundred yards away in the heap of rubble that used to be Jericho. He begins to think about how much he'd like to have some of those treasures so he slips out of his tent and quickly makes his way over to where the market place of that great city once stood. It's a bright moonlit night and he sees a reflection of something shiny. It's an overturned bag of precious silver and he grabs it. Why, there must be 200 shekels of silver here. This is more money than he ever had and he runs his fingers through it and thinks, "While I'm here, I should look for more." There was a wedge of gold. "How much could this be worth?"he thought as he pulled it to his chest. As he started out of the city, he sees something else. A beautiful robe imported from Babylon—a garment only royalty could afford. Overcome with greed, he clutches the robe as well. He gets back to his tent, pulls back the flooring and digs a hole to cover up his possessions. Surely he breathes a sigh of relief. "I've done it," he thought. "I've gotten away with it! No one saw me!" And no one did see him—except God.

How often that happens. People are secretly and clandestinely involved in doing things they know they should not be doing and they think no one knows. "No one saw me." But I'll tell you this, even when you conceal it and disguise it and cover it up flawlessly—God knows it and eventually we will all give an account for ourselves. Believe me, if we could interview Achan, he would tell us about the high cost of sin.

Notice with me the progression of this downward spiral. It began with a ***look***. *He* ***saw*** the spoils— the beautiful cloak, the 200 shekels, the gold wedge. The enticement and the attraction of the money and the beautiful robe captured his lustful eyes, which led Achan to declare, "I began to covet them." So the look quickly turned to ***lust***. There was nothing incriminating about the look, but the glance soon became a gaze and the gaze sparked the vulnerability of Achan's lustful heart. We read in Proverbs, "Hell and destruction are never full; so the eyes of man are never satisfied" (Proverbs 27:20, KJV).

The last commandment of the 10 commandments is broken here by Achan. God's law calls us to stay away from coveting things that don't belong to us. Covetousness, by definition, is the inordinate desire to have things that are not rightfully ours. It's the yearning that can grip your "Achan heart" and cause you to do things you shouldn't do. It's all to satisfy the carnal cravings of our flesh.

Finally, with Achan, we notice he saw, he coveted, he took and then he concealed and covered up his offense as he hid the spoils in his tent. When I read this downward spiral of covetousness, I think of King David who, one night in Jerusalem, noticed a beautiful lady bathing on her rooftop. After he looked he began to lust. He sent his messengers to get her and he committed adultery with her. Then in an effort to conceal it all, he took the life of her husband, Uriah. He saw, he coveted, he took, he concealed. What was true with Achan was true with Israel's greatest King. James concisely states this behavior, "But each person is tempted when he is drawn away and enticed by his own evil desires. Then after desire has conceived, it gives birth to sin, and when sin is fully grown, it gives birth to death" (James 1:14–15). James was telling Achan's story. More importantly, he may be telling your story because you've had a heart of covetousness, lusting for more or even lusting for someone else. But hear me…you can get out of this soon coming calamity. You can say with the Psalmist, "Turn away my eyes, oh God, from looking at worthless things—things that will not satisfy—things that will not fulfill—things that will kill, steal and destroy me."

We see in Achan a heart of covetousness but we see in God a hatred of compromise.

II. A HATRED OF COMPROMISE

The LORD then said to Joshua, "Stand up! Why are you on the ground? Israel has sinned. They have violated My covenant that I appointed for them. They have taken some of what was set apart. They have stolen, deceived, and put the things with their own belongings. This is why the Israelites cannot stand against their enemies. They will turn their backs and run from their enemies, because they have been set apart for destruction. I will no longer be with you unless you remove from you what is set apart. "Go and consecrate the people. Tell them to consecrate themselves tomorrow, for this is what the LORD, the God of Israel, says, 'There are among you, Israel, things set apart. You will not be able to stand against your enemies until you remove what is set apart. In the morning you must present your selves tribe by tribe. The tribe the LORD selects is to come forward clan by clan. The clan the LORD selects is to come forward family by family. The family the LORD selects is to come forward man by man. The one who is caught with the things set apart must be burned, along with everything he has, because he has violated the LORD's covenant and committed an outrage in Israel'.... So Joshua said to Achan, "My son, give glory to the LORD, the God of Israel, and make a confession to Him. I urge you, tell me what you have done. Don't hide anything from me." Achan replied to Joshua, "It is true. I have sinned against the LORD, the God of Israel..." (Joshua 7:10–15, 19–20)

Since our God is holy and righteous, He immensely disdains sin. He will not allow sin to go unpunished. You see, the first spiritual law isn't God loves you and has a wonderful plan for your life. No, it is God is angry at sin every day! He will not allow it to go unpunished. That's the necessity of the Incarnation. God's wrath was at a feverish pitch against fallen mankind. But instead of unleashing His judgment upon us the wretched and vile sinners, He sent His one and only son. II Corinthians 5:21 says it this way, "He made the One who did not know sin to be sin for us, so that we might become the righteousness of God in Him."

In that ignominious event at Calvary, Jesus bore our sin debt—the punishment for sin and the wrath of God's anger against sin. It fell vicariously on Him and now while God is still angry at sin every day, when you put your trust in Jesus and clothe yourself by faith in His righteousness, God's wrath is satisfied, His love is extended and forgiveness is enjoyed.

Here is what is going on in our text. God was clear about instructing His people not to take any of the accursed things. The spoils of Jericho were set apart for the treasury of God and it seems this one man's disobedience incriminated the entire nation. We read that in verse one. This became evident when going up to battle in Ai, a small insignificant outpost. The troops from Israel were attacked and scattered and 36 people lost their lives. So, God then tells Joshua to tell the people to consecrate themselves because I want to bring some divine accountability to each tribe, each clan, and each family until the perpetrator is uncovered. God says that when this man is found out he must be punished. He states what this appointed wrath will be to this loser and his family who've ignored his command.

After the call for consecration it was now time for the evaluation. So Joshua began bringing the various tribes before the Lord. Finally, from the tribe of Judah and the clan of Zerah, and from the family of Zabdi and Carmi comes Achan. Joshua says to him, "My son, give glory to God and make confession to Him. Tell me what you've done and don't hide anything from me." I don't know how Joshua knew who the guilty man was except the promise of God's word is this, "Be sure your sins will find you out!" Oh, you can hide sin for a while, for a short season, but ultimately it will come out of the closet and it will tell on you. Achan did confess his sin but it was too late. He was caught and here he would pay the penalty of sin as the Apostle Paul said in Romans 6:23, "For the wages of sin is death…"

But, imagine with me, if things would have been different. Imagine that if after taking the 200 shekels of silver, the wedge of gold and the Babylonian robe, that while he is sitting in his tent he begins to grieve about what he has done and he thinks to himself, "My God, what have I done? I have defied You!" Imagine that he decided to run to Joshua's tent and fall on his knees and say, "Joshua, I have taken these things that don't belong to me. I'm sorry. Please take them and put them in the treasury of the Lord." Imagine that he cried out to God for forgiveness. Do you think things would have been different? Sure. We have the principle in Proverbs, "He who covers his sins will not prosper, but whoever confesses and forsakes them will have mercy" (Proverbs 28:13, NKJV). That's the timeless truth. You can't cover your sin because "your Achan heart will tell on you." It's a paradox. If you cover your sin God will find it but if you uncover your sin God will cover it. God's mercy is NOT getting what you DO deserve. God's grace is giving you what you DON'T deserve. Those who call upon God receive grace, mercy and forgiveness.

What about the punishment of Achan's family? Certainly we would conclude that they were somehow involved in the cover up; that they were somehow involved in the concealment, and they were co-conspirators in this clandestine crime. We read in other occasions in the Old Testament, like Korah's rebellion and Haman's foiled conspiracy that the judgment and wrath extended beyond the individual to the family members as well, and so it was with Achan. God still has a hatred for compromise and while God's mercy and grace are available, it only extends to those who will repent and come home to God. Acts 3:19 says, "Therefore repent and turn back, that your sins may be wiped out so that seasons of refreshing may come from the presence of the Lord."

III. A HARVEST OF CONSEQUENCES

What can I say, Lord, now that Israel has turned its back and run from its enemies? When the Canaanites and all who live in the land hear about this, they will surround us and wipe out our name from the earth. Then what will You do about Your great name?.....Then Joshua and all Israel with him took Achan son of Zerah, the silver, the cloak, and the bar of gold, his sons and daughters, his ox, donkey, and sheep, his tent, and all that he had, and brought them up to the Valley of Achor. Joshua said, "Why have you troubled us? Today the LORD will trouble you!" So all Israel stoned them to death. They burned their bodies, threw stones on them, and raised over him a large pile of rocks that remains to this day. Then the LORD turned from His burning anger. Therefore that place is called the Valley of Achor to this day. (Joshua 7:8–9, 24–26)

You can't read this narrative without concluding just how high the consequences of sin are. The Prophet Hosea said, "For they have sown the wind, and they shall reap the whirlwind" (Hosea 8:7, KJV). So it was with Achan. But understand this, no one sins in a vacuum. There is a cause and effect. There are consequences for our actions and this story screams with the writer of Proverbs, "The way of the transgressor is hard!" Let's look at four consequences that resulted from this sin of covetousness.

A. Dishonored God

The name of Yahweh was dishonored by Achan's actions. Honestly, anytime our behavior compromises God's standards, we dishonor God's name. We can do that with our lips and we can do that with our life. I wonder with you, have you been dishonoring

God in your conversations? Have you dishonored Him in your decisions? Have you dishonored Him in your attitude? Have you dishonored Him in your ungratefulness? Have you dishonored Him in your dishonesty? God wants His name esteemed and honored.

A couple of hundred years before the birth of Christ, Alexander the Great conquered the known world. It was said that at 33 years of age he sat and wept because there were no other countries and providences left to conquer. Alexander heard about the misbehavior of one of his soldiers and went personally to the young general and began to reprimand him for his cowardly ways, his rebellious spirit and his unwillingness to follow orders. The story is told that at the end of the reprimand, Alexander said, "Soldier, what is your name?" "Alexander" responded the soldier. Alexander the Great said, "Either change your name or change your ways, for you've dishonored my name." Whenever we speak unkindly; when we behave unseemingly; when we are full of bitterness and have hearts full of covetousness, we dishonor the name of our God.

B. Defeat to God's People

Israel now couldn't stand against a small band of renegades at Ai. Here's the deal for us as believers—we're in this thing together. We are all part of the body of Christ and as one drop of poison can kill the whole body, so it is with sin. We're not independent. We're interdependent. I Corinthians 12:12 says, "For as the body is one and has many parts, and all the parts of that body, though many, are one body—so is Christ."

In our story, 36 people lost their lives, three from every tribe, because of Achan's sin. The first military defeat was experienced because of one man's disobedience. This principle is why we as a church must keep sin out of the body. Even though it is with one or two people, it's like a cancer. It destroys us all. It's like hitting your thumb with a hammer. The pain is not confined to the thumb. Your whole body hurts.

Church members need to help each other, no matter what church you belong to. We need to encourage one another to stay the course and to live lives that are pleasing and acceptable to our God, lest we bring condemnation upon our wonderful churches and the entire body of Christ.

C. Disgraced His Parents

Three times in this chapter we discover a listing of Achan's family. He was the son of Carmi and even his grandparents and great grandparents are mentioned. Undoubtedly, the shame extended its ugly head to generations. It's a pretty sad scenario when we disgrace our parents by our behavior. Most of you know I'm from a small town in Oklahoma. My home town had about 17,000 people at the time that I was growing up there. It was my parents' home, my grandparents' home, and my great-grandparents' home. Four generations lived within a five mile radius. In that context, a person's reputation is everything. I didn't want to do anything that might reflect negatively on the Dighton family. I never wanted to disgrace my parents. The fifth commandment says, "Honor your father and mother" and with it there's the promise that you might live a long life. Conversely, Achan's life was cut sadly short. He disgraced his parents and brought defeat to the people of God and dishonored the name of God. But that's not all.

D. Death to His Children

All we can conclude is that Achan's sons and daughters were co-conspirators with him—accomplices to the deadly crime. When he took the accursed things, they surely must have been involved in the cover up.

I can't think of anything anymore vile than corrupting your own children. Many parents do though, maybe not intentionally, but sometimes it is through the parents neglect that their children are corrupted. Jesus warned, "It would be better for him if a millstone were hung around his neck and he were thrown into the sea than for him to cause one of these little ones to stumble" (Luke 17:2).

That day near a place that one day would be called the City of Palms; Achan played the fool and became the loser. It all started innocently enough. No one was going to benefit from the silver or gold or that beautiful Babylonian garment, so Achan concluded that he could have it for himself. A look turned to lust. He stole the accursed items and concealed them. While he thought it was safely secured in the floor of his tent, God, who has a hatred for compromise and disobedience, was coming after him and soon he would pay the high cost of his sin.

So what can we learn from this defeat and disaster? Surely, there are some lessons to be gleaned and indeed there are.

1. Sin always has a high price.

It seems throughout the word of God we discover this resounding truth: Sin—

- It will always take you farther than you want to ***stray***
- It will always keep you longer than you want to ***stay***
- It will always cost you more than you want to ***pay***

All of this was true with Achan and it will be true with you, as well.

2. God is faithful to His word.

- The clear and clarion call from God was "Don't take these items or else you will pay the consequences". As surely as God is faithful in His love, He is faithful in His judgment as well.

Galatians 6:7–8 says, "Don't be deceived: God is not mocked. For whatever a man sows he will also reap, because the one who sows to his flesh will reap corruption from the flesh, but the one who sows to the Spirit will reap eternal life from the Spirit."

3. The influence we have with our lives is critical. Achan's sin—

- Cost 36 people their lives
- Caused the first defeat of God's people in Canaan
- Shamed his parents and grandparents
- Brought about the execution of his own children

Chapter Four

A Legendary Loser

I Samuel 17

I. A PRIDEFUL PROPOSITION
   A. An Imposing Presence
   B. The Intimidating Rhetoric
   C. An Increasing Persistence

II. A PREPOSTEROUS PROMISE
   A. Proven Faith
   B. Poised Faith
   C. Prudent Faith

III. A PREEMINENT PURPOSE
   A. Our Salvation
   B. Our Satisfaction
   C. Our Sanctification

Undoubtedly, one of the most well-known Bible stories in the entire Bible is the story of David and Goliath. The reason we love it so is because the underdog defeats the favorite. It's a classic battle of good versus evil with the hope of overcoming all odds and winning. This David and Goliath analogy was used by Bishop Eddie Long in his mega church, New Birth Missionary Baptist Church, outside of Atlanta. As you know, Bishop Long had been accused by three young men in his church of being sexually involved with them and coercing them by lavishing gifts on them to have sex with him. But Long said this battle he is up against is like David against Goliath, implying he is the overwhelming underdog in these accusations. All I can say is this—if he is guilty, then shame on him for associating himself with the shepherd king of Israel and lying about his perversions. I Samuel 17 is the story of David and Goliath. It's the story of a little winner and a big loser.

I. A PRIDEFUL PROPOSITION

The Philistines gathered their forces for war at Socoh in Judah and camped between Socoh and Azekah in Ephes-dam-mim. Saul and the men of Israel gathered and camped in the Valley of Elah; then they lined up in battle formation to face the Philistines. The Philistines were standing on one hill, and the Israelites were standing on another hill with a ravine between them. Then a champion named Goliath, from Gath, came out from the Philistine camp. He was nine feet, nine inches tall and wore a bronze helmet and bronze scale armor that weighed 125 pounds. There was bronze armor on his shins, and a bronze sword was slung between his shoulders. His spear shaft was like a weaver's beam, and the iron point of his spear weighed 15 pounds. In addition, a shield-bearer was walking in front of him. He stood and shouted to the Israelite battle formations: "Why do you come out to line up in battle formation?" He asked them, "Am I not a Philistine and are you not servants of Saul? Choose one of your men and have him come down against me. If he wins in a fight against me and kills me, we will be your servants. But if I win against him and kill him, then you will be our servants and serve us." Then the Philistine said, "I defy the ranks of Israel today. Send me a man so we can fight each other!" When Saul and all Israel heard these words from the Philistine, they lost their courage and were terrified. Now David was the son of the Ephrathite from Bethlehem of Judah named Jesse. Jesse had eight sons and during Saul's reign was already an old man. Jesse's three oldest sons had followed Saul to the war, and their names were Eliab, the firstborn, Abinadab, the next, and Shammah, the third, and David was the youngest. The three oldest had followed Saul, but David kept going back and forth from Saul to tend his father's flock in Bethlehem. Every morning and evening for 40 days the Philistine came forward and took his stand. (I Samuel 17:1–16)

We're introduced to Goliath from Gath here in Chapter 17 and he obviously is confident and cocky. You read his boastful proposition to the army of Israel and it quickly becomes obvious that his pores are oozing with pride and arrogance. While he is gigantic in physical stature, he has an ego to match his magnitude. From Genesis to Revelation God's word puts out a warning about pride. Proverbs 16:18 says, "Pride comes before destruction, and an arrogant spirit before a fall." This would soon be the plight of this Philistine giant.

Actually, if you study the history of pride you'll discover it predates Adam and Eve and was the first sin ever committed. It happened before God spoke this world into existence because pride was at the root of Lucifer's rebellion. Satan himself was cast down because of his prideful heart. You remember in Isaiah 14:13–14, the motivation behind Satan's rebellion is exposed as he declared, "…I will ascend into heaven, I will exalt my throne above the stars of God… I will be like the Most High" (NKJV). This powerful angelic creature, possessing beauty and glory far beyond our comprehension arrogantly desired recognition and status equal to God Himself. In response, God swiftly and severely judged him.

Pride not only appears to be the earliest sin, but it is at the core of all sin. "Pride", John Stott writes, "is more than the first of the seven deadly sins; it is itself the essence of all sin."[6] Here we see Goliath, full of pride, strutting around, yet prophetically he would soon bite the dust because that's where pride eventually leaves any person. Let's look at three things about this giant loser.

A. An Imposing Presence

We're told about the size of this mammoth man. The King James Version says he was six cubits and a span. A cubit was eighteen inches and a span was nine inches. So Goliath stood nearly ten feet tall! The tallest player ever to play in the NBA was Manute Bol, who just recently passed away. Manute was 7'7" tall. If you can imagine Goliath was 2'2" taller than that Sudanese skyscraper. The big difference was Manute only weighed what Goliath's armor weighed, which was 125 pounds.

Goliath indeed had an imposing presence and it brought fear not only to the army of Israel, but according to verse 11, to King Saul who was also greatly afraid. Fear has been called the greatest enemy of human potential because more people are held back by fear than any other factor.

I recently read that we're all born with two inherent fears:

- Fear of falling
- Fear of loud noises

But as you know, as we grow older, those two fears are soon parlayed into 1,000's of fears and that's where God's people were living here in Elah. They were living in fear. Chuck Swindoll said, "The only sound being heard in the Israelite camp was the knocking of knees and the chattering of teeth."[7] I wonder if any of you would say you are beset by fear. Are you afraid of what might be about to happen? Fear is the natural response when you focus on your problems rather than on God. But we see more in our text than just Goliath's imposing presence.

B. The Intimidating Rhetoric

Goliath is throwing down the gauntlet and is basically saying, "I want a challenge. Give me your meanest and most menacing man. After I take him down, we'll cart the rest of you cowards off into captivity." You talk about a bully! Goliath was the original prototype. Bullying is now a big problem in schools and also in the workplace across America. I read some interesting observations about bullies.

1. They have personalities that are authoritarian and have a need to control and dominate.

2. They are usually arrogant and narcissistic. They have quickness to anger and use of force. Sometimes their behavior is driven by insecurity and envy, hoping to boost their low self esteem.

3. They have a much higher chance to become incarcerated in the future, than the population at large.

Let me just say…I hate bullies. I hate their behavior that preys on someone who is weaker or frail. It's not a new phenomenon. It was pervasive back in the 60's when I was growing up, and I've always despised that behavior.

One of the wonderful traits about our Savior is His love for the oppressed, underprivileged, the weak and the weary. Isaiah 43:3, speaking of the soon coming Savior, says, "He will not break a bruised reed, and He will not put out a smoldering wick; He will faithfully bring justice."

C. An Increasing Persistence

For 40 days, morning and evening, this taunting, bullying, obnoxious monologue persisted as Goliath brazenly insulted God's people. No doubt he had put God's people to the test. In the scriptures the number 40 is often used as a sign of testing.

1. It was true with Moses, after killing an Egyptian. For 40 years God tested him on the back side of Midian tending sheep before He would use him to be His deliverer.

2. It was true with Joshua and Caleb, too. They wandered with God's people for 40 years in the wilderness after bringing their favorable report. But it was God's plan for them to wait 4 decades before He allowed them to go in and occupy the Promised Land.

3. And let's not forget about Jesus. For 40 days in the Judean wilderness near Qumran, Jesus was put to the test by Satan.

This had been a time of testing for the Israelites. They had been bullied by Goliath who really was nothing more than a loser that was about to be taken down by an unsuspecting shepherd boy with faith in God and a willingness to engage the enemy. Because when fear knocked on this young shepherd boys heart faith answered and discovered that no one was there.

II. A PREPOSTEROUS PROMISE

David answered Saul, "Your servant has been tending his father's sheep. Whenever a lion or a bear came and carried off a lamb from the flock, I went after it, struck it down, and rescued the lamb from its mouth. If it reared up against me, I would grab it by its fur, strike it down, and kill it. Your servant has killed lions and bears; this uncircumcised Philistine will be like one of them, for he has defied the armies of the living God." Then David said, "The LORD who rescued me from the paw of the lion and the paw of the bear will rescue me from the hand of this Philistine." Saul said to David, "Go, and may the LORD be with you." Then Saul had his own military clothes put on David. He put a bronze helmet on David's head and had him put on armor. David strapped his sword on over the military clothes and tried to walk, but he was not used to them. "I can't walk in these," David said to Saul, "I'm not used to them."So David took them off. Instead, he took his staff in his hand and chose five smooth stones from the wadi and put them in the pouch, in his shepherd's bag. Then, with his sling in his hand, he approached the Philistine. The Philistine came closer and closer to David, with the shield-bearer in front of him. When the Philistine looked and saw David, he despised him because he was just a youth, healthy and handsome. He said to David, "Am I a dog that you come against me with sticks?" Then he cursed David by his gods. "Come here," the Philistine called to David, "and I'll give your flesh to the birds of the sky and the wild beasts!" David said to the Philistine, "You come against me with a dagger, spear, and sword, but I come against you in the name of the LORD of Hosts, the God of Israel's armies—you have defied Him. Today, the LORD will hand you over to me. Today, I'll strike you down, cut your head off, and give the corpses of the Philistine camp to the birds of the sky and the creatures of the earth. Then all the world will know that Israel has a God," (I Samuel 17:34–46)

David is sent on a mission by his father, Jesse, to check on his three older brothers who were encamped in Elah with Saul's army. His mission was to bring them some food. David showed up and witnessed the debacle and the fear and intimidation in the Israelite army and he was blown away by the cowering down of his fellow Jews. Then David, unlike the rest of his peers, made what can only be called a *Preposterous Promise.* He says, "I'll go fight that uncircumcised Philistine who has defied God and embarrassed our country men."But then David calls a sidebar and says "Now tell me—if I defeat this loudmouth giant, what will it get me?"He is told the prize is:

1. Saul's beautiful daughter

2. He will be given great riches, and

3. He will be tax exempt

David says, "I'm on my way!" As you would expect, Saul tried to stop him and says, "You can't go fight this Philistine. You're just a youth, and he's been a warrior since he was young" (I Sam. 17:33). Here's the tension. Saul operated in fear and David operated in faith. He said, "I'm going in Jehovah's power. God will see me through and bring victory." Fear looks at the problem. It says, "God, you're not able here." But faith looks past the problem and says, "God, while I don't know how…I know you." Fear focuses on what can go wrong and faith believes in the one who can make things right. Here is how David could make such a *Preposterous Promise;* he wasn't going to rely upon his strength, his sufficiency, his prowess, but upon God's strength, God's sufficiency and God's omnipotence.

When you study the life of David, there is a word that is the banner over his life and that word is *faith*. If you read in Hebrews 11, the great Hall of Fame of Faith, you'll find David along with others who, through faith, subdued Kingdoms, obtained promises, quenched violence, escaped the edge of the sword and get this—"gained strength after being weak….the world was not worthy of them" (Heb. 11:34, 38). David was a man of faith and that's why he would be called a man after God's own heart. Hebrews 11:6 tells us, "Now without faith it is impossible to please God, for the one who draws near to Him must believe that He exists and rewards those who seek Him." I want you to notice with me the following three things about David's faith.

A. Proven Faith

The lion and bear had been no problem. God delivered him in that remote and secluded setting and He will do the same on the center stage here in the Valley of Elah. Don't miss this; David was now exercising what he'd been practicing for years. It was his way of life. He trusted in God and what he'd known alone and in private, he was about to do in this most memorable arena. Honestly, that's the way it can be with you. Trust God privately and in the smaller things and when you face a great obstacle or a giant problem, as with David, you'll be ready because you too will have a *Proven Faith.*

B. Poised Faith

Saul had a solution and it was for David to put on his armor and use it. But David said, "This will never work" and he refused the King's armor and his ideas on how he should proceed. I submit to you, Saul's advice is the advice of the world. Proverbs 16:25 teaches us that, "There is a way that seems right to a man, but in the end it is the way of death." If you are dealing with problems and predicaments, the world will definitely throw you a solution. They will convince you that what you need is a:

- Drink—drown your sorrows with hard liquor and you'll be better. But each drink takes you further and further into darkness and destruction.
- The world will convince those of you who are having marriage problems that divorce is the best option.
- You'll hear that sexual promiscuity is fun and freeing, but it will take you to brokenness and despair.

Saul had a solution for David's encounter and the world will have a pseudo-solution for you in whatever you are up against. Colossians 2:8 says, "Beware lest any man spoil you through philosophy and vain deceit, after the tradition of men, after the rudiments of the world, and not after Christ" (KJV). The question for you is this—will you remain poised and confident when the temptation of what the world has to offer is presented to you? Will you say with me, "I know whom I have believed and am persuaded that He is able, to keep that which I've committed unto Him against that day" (II Tim. 1:12, KJV).

C. Prudent Faith

David knew it was neither by his own might nor power, but by God's enablement that would give him the victory so he went down to the creek and selected five smooth stones. The reason for the five stones has been debated over the years. Some have argued that they represented the five major Philistine cities of Gath, Ekron, Ashdod, Gaza and Ashkelon. Others said Goliath had four brothers. All of these things are nothing more than conjecture. I submit to you that David wasn't presumptuous, but he was prudent. He wanted to be well prepared. Faith is not illogical or unfounded. He was trusting in God, but he wanted to be well prepared.

Our faith in God doesn't demand we check our brains at the door, but it's well founded—anchored not in speculation but in revelation. It causes us not to respond impulsively or capriciously, but prudently. As God said, "Come now, and let us reason together says the Lord" (Isa. 1:18, NKJV).

David had a faith that I am envious of. While others looked at the enormity of the enemy, he looked to the strength and the sufficiency and the sovereignty of his Savior. Understand this; our faith doesn't bring the victory. Our faith is the victory. While we're looking at Life's Losers, the common bond in all of them is this—they didn't have faith in God. The Apostle John tells us, "For whatever is born of God overcomes the world. And this is the victory that has overcome the world: our faith. Who is he who overcomes the world but he who believes that Jesus is the Son of God?" (I John 5:4–5, NKJV).

Today all your years of losing, all your years of disappointments and shame, all your past failures and mistakes can be forgotten and forgiven if you will simply believe. It's as the songwriter said, "Faith is the victory that overcomes the world."[8]

III. A PREEMINENT PURPOSE

"and the whole assembly will know that it is not by sword or by spear that the LORD saves, for the battle is the LORD's. He will hand you over to us." When the Philistine started forward to attack him, David ran quickly to the battle line to meet the Philistine." (I Samuel 17:47–48)

David said the reason and the divine purpose for this victory that's about to transpire is to show the world that Yahweh is supreme because all the glory is going to Him. He is saying, "I am not taking on this giant by myself. I'm going to demonstrate that God is able to take anything and anyone, regardless of their stature and size and reduce them to dust. The *Preeminent Purpose* of this battle will be to lift up and glorify the only true God. Three things quickly come to mind about how you and I can bring glory to God.

A. Our Salvation

In John 17, as Jesus agonizes in that high intercessory prayer the night of His crucifixion he declares, "This is eternal life: that they may know You, the only true God, and the One You have sent—Jesus Christ. I have glorified You on the earth by completing the work You gave Me to do. Now, Father, glorify Me in Your presence with that glory I had with you before the world existed" (John 17:3–5). Jesus was on a mission and he wanted the glory for the Father and for himself. The purpose of our salvation is not just about getting to heaven, but it is about glorifying the one who made it all possible.

B. Our Satisfaction

"In Your presence is fullness of joy; at your right hand are pleasures forevermore" (Psalm 16:11, NKJV). John Piper says, "God is most glorified in you when you're most satisfied in Him."[9] As long as you see living for God as a burden, drudgery and something merely to be endured, then God will never be glorified in your life. Conversely, if in your life there is joy unspeakable and it is full of glory then rest assured—Jesus is exalted and honored. So I'm asking you this—is Jesus enough for you? Or are you discontent and always wanting more? Remember, God is most glorified in you when you are most satisfied in Him.

C. Our Sanctification

The way we glorify God is by remaining on the straight and narrow path that leads to life. When our lives are holy, consecrated, abhorring what is evil and clinging to that which is good, living above reproach, possessing a right and grateful attitude, we glorify God. I Corinthians 6:20 says, "for you were bought at a price; therefore glorify God in your body." Once again we are learning a lesson from one of Life's Losers and I'm saying to you—you can lose out if you miss the purpose of God for your life. But you become a winner if you will live by faith.

Chapter Five

A Lethal Loser

I Samuel 21, 22; Psalm 52

I. A DREADFUL MISFORTUNE

A. Fabrication
B. Accommodations
C. Notation

II. A DESTRUCTIVE MOUTH

A. Boastful
B. Belligerent
C. Blasphemous

III. A DEVILISH MURDER

A. Saul's Revenge
B. Servant's Refusal
C. David's Response

When you study the life of King David, you'll discover that he was a unique man. And while we're often perplexed by his behavior, not appearing at all to be a man after God's own heart, still his love for God and pursuit of God was his mainstay. One of the endearing traits about David was his compassion and love for those who ridiculed and even rebelled against him—men like King Saul and Absalom, who had as their mission the goal of taking him down. But still love won out and David demonstrated a Christ-like response to them. Yet, while that was David's demeanor most of the time, it wasn't true in every sense because there was a man from Edom, a soldier and keeper of Saul's sheep, that David would come to despise—and rightfully so. His name was Doeg.

We read his story in I Samuel 21 and 22. But David also penned Psalms 52 which nails this loser and reveals to us the way of this torturous transgressor. So now we see Doeg get in line with our growing list of losers—Cain, Judas, Achan and Goliath. Our goal is to consider the foolishness and the error of his ways, so that we will guard our steps and not fall into foolish temptation.

Losers come in all shapes and sizes. Webster says, "A loser is one who comes to destruction or ruin; one who goes astray, becomes bewildered. They fall behind. They fail to win."[10] As you might expect, losers even have their own website (losers.org) and the search list references dorks, freaks, Goths, greenies, groupies, nerds, punks, rednecks, treckkies and wannabe's. While those identify a subculture that we identify as losers, still the list is more inclusive than that because a loser is anyone who misses out on all that God has for us as believers in Jesus Christ.

I. A DREADFUL MISFORTUNE

David went to Ahimelech the priest at Nob. Ahimelech was afraid to meet David, so he said to him, "Why are you alone and no one is with you?" David answered Ahimelech the priest, "The king gave me a mission, but he told me, 'Don't let anyone know anything about the mission I'm sending you on or what I have ordered you to do.' I have stationed my young men at a certain place. Now what do you have on hand? Give me five loaves of bread or whatever can be found." The priest told him, "There is no ordinary bread on hand. However, there is consecrated bread, but the young men may eat it only if they have kept themselves from women." David answered him, "I swear that women are being kept from us, as always when I go out to battle. The young men's bodies are consecrated even on an ordinary mission, so of course their bodies are consecrated today." So the priest gave him the consecrated bread, for there was no bread there except the bread of the Presence that had been removed from before the LORD. When the bread was removed, it had been replaced with warm bread. One of Saul's servants, detained before the LORD, was there that day. His name was Doeg the Edomite, chief of Saul's shepherds. David said to Ahimelech, "Do you have a spear or sword on hand? I didn't even bring my sword or my weapons since the king's mission was urgent." The priest replied, "The sword of Goliath the Philistine, whom you killed in the valley of Elah, is here, wrapped in a cloth behind the ephod. If you want to take it for yourself, then take it, for there isn't another one here." "There's none like it!" David said, "Give it to me." (I Samuel 21:1–9)

In I Samuel 21, we find David on the run from King Saul and he comes to a place called Nob, located on Mt. Scopus. It was known as the City of Priests. There he encountered a priest named Ahimelech, who was the grandson of Eli. He seems to be afraid to meet with David. The reason being, he's heard that King Saul is in pursuit of him. Since David is a fugitive, any help might appear to be an act of insurrection against Saul. The reputation of Saul's crazed and maniac behavior was well known and Ahimelech didn't want the wrath of the King turned against him for assisting David.

A. Fabrication

David, in desperation, fabricates a story to imply that he was there because he was on a secret mission from King Saul and he couldn't share any of the details. Ahimelech is gullible and he agrees to give some assistance to David and his men. This is an unfortunate commentary on the winsome and charismatic personality of Jesse's son as here he embellishes the truth for his own gain.

B. Accommodations

David asked the priest if he could give them some bread because both he and his men were hungry. Ahimelech says, "All we have is the consecrated bread from the Tabernacle." This is known as the Shewbread or the Bread of Presence. You will remember, that this is the bread from the Holy Place where there are twelve loaves representing the twelve tribes of Israel. As was customary, it was exchanged weekly for fresh bread. So, David says his soldiers are ceremoniously clean meaning they haven't had sexual relations.

Whether this is true or not is uncertain, but seeing that David had just lied about his mission, he might have been lying about his men as well.

Proverbs 14:25 says, "A truthful witness rescues lives, but one who utters lies is deceitful" David's fabrications are going to set in motion a *Dreadful Misfortune.* He would later take responsibility for the carnage that would soon take place here in Nob. Ahimelech would also go on to give to David the sword of Goliath that resided in the Tabernacle as well, so that David would have some protection.

C. Notation

Now we are introduced to our main character; Doeg the Edomite, who was one of Saul's chief shepherds. He had been detained at the Tabernacle. So, for some reason, this vicious and vindictive renegade is still there—no doubt doing some form of penance and something punitive for a previous offense he had committed. Whatever that was, it would pale in comparison to the guilt he would have after his soon slaughter of 85 priests. No wonder when David wrote Psalm 52 about this Edomite shepherd, the first word that came to his mind was **evil**. We will see that the vileness and licentiousness of his depravity would soon be revealed.

I wonder…why didn't he learn a lesson with his detention? He had just paid the price for his lawlessness, yet no lesson was learned and no change was ever evident. It only spurred him on to more grievous offenses. That is the problem with the overcrowding of prisons in America. They're saturated with repeat offenders. I recently read that 6% of criminals commit 70% of all crimes. 68% of men arrested are repeat offenders and 58% of women. 7 out of 10 inmates released from being incarcerated are back in jail within three years. Doesn't anybody ever learn from their experiences? Honestly, these repeat offenses are not just a criminal and legal problem. I have a feeling it's your problem as well if you refuse to learn from your mistakes, your failures and your bad choices.

Our goal in studying this series of Losers is to learn Life's Lessons from wrong decisions by others. Why? So we won't make them, too. Shame on us, if we don't learn along the way, that our selfish, senseless poor choices will lead us astray. Proverbs 24:32 says, "I saw, and took it to heart; I looked, and received instruction:" Let's not be like Doeg, whose detention only led to more incriminating behavior. Instead, let's make it a goal, as we read about each one of these Life's Loser's, to ask God to reveal one thing that we might learn and immediately apply it to our lives.

II. A DESTRUCTIVE MOUTH

Why brag about evil, you hero! God's faithful love is constant. Like a sharpened razor, your tongue devises destruction, working treachery. You love evil instead of good, lying instead of speaking truthfully. You love any words that destroy, you treacherous tongue! This is why God will bring you down forever. He will take you, ripping you out of your tent; He will uproot you from the land of the living. The righteous will look on with awe and will ridicule him: "Here is the man who would not make God his refuge, but trusted in the abundance of his riches, taking refuge in his destructive behavior." (Psalm 52:1–7)

This Davidic Psalm was penned by David after Doeg had "ratted him out" to Saul and set in motion the coming calamity at Nob. While it is obvious that David greatly disdains Doeg, he says that the thing he despises most about the guy is his mouth! While his heart is evil and wicked, his issues don't stay contained there. No he keeps revealing the depravity of his heart with his lips. I am reminded of Solomon's teaching about good words, "For they are life to those who find them, and health to all their flesh. Keep your heart with all diligence, for out of it spring the issues of life" (Prov. 4:22–23, NKJV).

A. Boastful

In the last chapter about Goliath we learned that pride and arrogance are abominations to God. We are also going to learn that pride is at the root of all sin. This perversion had augured even deeper because Doeg is boasting in evil. Verse 3 tells us Doeg loved evil instead of good. The thought conveyed in the Hebrew word for brag is not necessarily someone strutting around making boastful claims about themselves, as with Goliath. But this is a smug and twisted superiority that delights in the ruin of others.

Sometimes people boast to cover up their insecurity but Doeg's arrogance was darker and more demonic than that. He prided himself in his caustic and carnal cravings. He was arrogant and boastful, like a serial murderer proud of his merciless killings. Hugh Latimer said, "If you need to boast about your sin, you haven't accomplished much." Shame on the man or woman who boasts about their depravity!

B. Belligerent

David says of Doeg, "Your tongue is like a razor, cutting people to shreds." A sharp tongue is a common metaphor for destructive speech. Verse 4 says, "You love any words that destroy, you treacherous tongue." Sometimes we think of people who have a problem with their tongue as primarily having a problem with not guarding their speech. What pops into their head comes immediately out of their mouth. Certainly, the Bible warns against that. We're to be quick to hear and slow to speak. But with Doeg, it seems his destructive, disparaging and deranged words were stored for just the right occasion.

The end of I Samuel 21 tells of David's escape to King Achish, one of the rulers of the Philistines. At the start of Chapter 22 it tells of David gathering his mighty men around him in the stronghold at Adullam. Both of these events intervene between the time Doeg saw David with Ahimelech in Nob and when he reported it to Saul. So it wasn't that Doeg just blocked out what he had seen at the first opportunity. On the contrary, he had a piece of valuable information and he kept it to himself until it could do the most harm and would best serve his interests. As soon as Saul mentioned that none of his informers were concerned about him or told him anything, Doeg in a boastful and belligerent way spoke up to say, "Here's what I saw."He then proceeded to tell of Ahimelech's help to David.

Have you ever known anyone who is always looking for an opportunity to rat on someone? We used to call them a tattletale. The word "tattletale" has it's etymology in the German word "talo" which means talk or to speak. When the compound word was put together in the 15th century it spoke of someone who betrays secrets or loves to tell on others and the word tattletale has stuck. Here is what I know—rarely are tattletales embraced by their peers; their schoolmates. You can rest assured that Doeg was no different. His tongue was arrogant, prideful and insulting. He was boastful and belligerent and undoubtedly you could count his friends on one hand. Colossians 4:6 says, "Your speech should always be gracious, seasoned with salt" but it was not so with Doeg. He was boastful. He was belligerent. But unfortunately it doesn't end there.

C. Blasphemous

Blasphemy is when someone says or does anything that is irreverent toward God and held sacred by God. I ask you this—is there anything more irreverent and blasphemous than killing those who serve in sacred positions of the ministry of the Lord? That's why David is evoking judgment upon this evil Edomite.

Remember what David said when he had opportunity to repay Saul for his attempts to kill him? "I would not stretch out my hand against the LORD's anointed" (I Samuel 26:23, NKJV). David refused to repay evil for evil, but Doeg was repaying evil for the good that Ahimelech and the priests of God had done. David writes, "This man has rejected God. He will not make God his refuge."

Blasphemy of the Holy Spirit is, in one sense, the failure to flee to God to find forgiveness and refuge. By definition it is the continual, perpetual and final rejection of Jesus Christ as Savior. That's the ministry of the Holy Spirit—to point people to Jesus. When you reject the Lord Jesus Christ, not just once, but continually and perpetually, with a hardened heart and blinded eyes, you seal your fate. In the final day you will be compared with men like Doeg and Judas Iscariot and the thousands upon thousands who neglect so great a salvation.

Understand that what we do with our mouth is critical. It gives indication of a transformed heart. In Romans we read, "If you confess with your mouth, "Jesus is Lord," and believe in your heart that God raised Him from the dead, you will be saved. With the heart one believes, resulting in righteousness and with the mouth one confesses, resulting in salvation" (Romans 10:9–10). Know this—God will forgive every foul and sinful thing that ever escaped your mouth. Every lie, every curse word, every hateful thing you've said, every threat, every shameful and sinful thing. I John 1:9 says, "If we confess our sins, He is faithful and righteous to forgive us our sins and to cleanse us from all unrighteousness." But if you are unwilling to repent and believe it will be your undoing.

III. A DEVILISH MURDER

The king sent messengers to summon Ahimelech the priest, son of Ahitub, and his father's whole family, who were priests in Nob. All of them came to the king. Then Saul said, "Listen, son of Ahitub!" "I'm at your service, my lord," he said. Saul asked him, "Why did you and Jesse's son conspire against me? You gave him bread and a sword and inquired of God for him, so he could rise up against me and wait in ambush, as is the case today." Ahimelech replied to the king: "Who among all your servants is as faithful as David? He is the king's son-in-law, captain of your bodyguard, and honored in your house. Was today the first time I inquired of God for him? Of course not! Please don't let the king make an accusation against your servant or any of my father's household, for your servant didn't have any idea about all this." But the king said, "You will die, Ahimelech—you and your father's whole family!" Then the king ordered the guards standing by him, "Turn and kill the priests of the LORD because they sided with David. For they knew he was fleeing, but they didn't tell me." But the king's servants would not lift a hand to execute the priests of the LORD. So the king said to Doeg, "Go and execute the priests!" So Doeg the Edomite went and executed the priests himself. On that day, he killed 85 men who wore linen ephods. He also struck down Nob, the city of the priests, with the sword—both men and women, children and infants, oxen, donkeys, and sheep. However, one of the sons of Ahimelech son of Ahitub escaped. His name was Abiathar, and he fled to David. Abiathar told David that Saul had killed the priests of the LORD. Then David said to Abiathar, "I knew that Doeg the Edomite was there that day and that he was sure to report to Saul. I myself am responsible for the lives of everyone in your father's family. Stay with me. Don't be afraid, for the one who wants to take my life wants to take your life. You will be safe with me." (I Samuel 22:11–23)

King Saul sent messengers to Nob to bring Ahimelech to stand before him. Notice with me the conclusion of this heart wrenching narrative.

A. Saul's Revenge

Saul, in his customary crazed and capricious way, condemns Ahimelech and his family. It was as if Saul said, "Don't confuse me with the facts. I have an obsession to kill David and anyone standing in my way will die too." His revenge was so toxic, troubling and audacious that his own servants would not follow his commands.

B. Servant's Refusal

The most trusted men in Saul's army said, "We're not doing it." Saul knew whose heart was wicked enough to pull off the blasphemous execution and guess who he calls on? Doeg—whose name meant "timid or anxious". But he was unlike most of the names from antiquity as most fulfilled their name. Doeg, however; was aggressive and ruthless and while these sensible and sober-minded servants of Saul said, "No! We will not do this", Doeg gladly and glibly volunteered for this heinous murder.

C. David's Response

David said, "I knew all along that when that loser named Doeg saw what happened in Nob, he would run to Saul and this would be the result." While the Bible doesn't tell us what happened to Doeg, rabbinic tradition says that God sent three angels of destruction and one took away his learning, another buried his soul, while the other scattered his ashes over Mt. Scopus. While that is nothing more than rabbinic tradition, God's word does tell about the judgment of Doeg in Psalm 52. David has written that "God will bring you down forever, snatch you out of your tent". The word picture here is of a tent, the place where a family dwells, being uprooted by strong winds. Doeg and his family would be expunged from Israel. This is the promise of God to those who go the way of Doeg the Edomite, "the one who sows to his flesh will reap corruption from the flesh, but the one who sows to the Spirit will reap eternal life from the Spirit" (Galatians 6:8).

Chapter Six

The Loser's Lot for Lying to God

Acts 5:1–11

I. A CONTRAST IN GIVING
   A. An Act of Devotion
   B. An Act of Deception

II. A CONDEMNATION FROM GOD
   A. Spiritual Perception
   B. Serious Punishment

III. THE CONSEQUENCE OF GRIEF
   A. A Fearful Emotion
   B. A Flourishing Expansion

In the last five chapters we have been exploring together a variety of personalities that we have collectively called "losers". Up until now, they have all been men, but there are several bad girls of the Bible as well—so, ladies, you are not exempt. In the coming chapters, we're going to look at Jezebel and Herodias, but today it's not just a lady who gets this unfortunate and unflattering tag—it's a couple—a husband and wife.

The story of this infamous couple is found in Acts 5 and their names are Ananias and Sapphira. This husband and wife received one of the swiftest, most somber and severe judgments ever documented in the New Testament. While the judgments of God are past finding out, this one does leave us scratching our heads, wondering why God took their lives. Or even more concerning and applicable, why did God judge them so harshly and still overlook the sin and hypocrisy in our lives? Indeed, God has preserved this story for a reason and surely it is this—that we might see the holiness of our God, His wrath that accompanies disobedience, and also that we might know that He is serious about personal hypocrisy and pretentiousness from His people.

I, recently read about a father and son, Gary and Brian Rickert, who were developers in one of the suburbs in St. Louis. They were sent to prison for lying about their finances. It seems they submitted false documentation to three loan institutions so that they might receive $5 million for a real estate development–but they got caught. They were sentenced to six years in the federal prison for defrauding three banks. They proved that lying about your finances has serious implications. Ananias and Sapphira proved that when you lie to God about your finances, the judgment can be much harsher than six years in prison.

I. A CONTRAST IN GIVING

But a man named Ananias, with Sapphira his wife, sold a piece of property. However, he kept back part of the proceeds with his wife's knowledge, and brought a portion of it and laid it at the apostles' feet. (Acts 5:1–2)

Acts 5 is a continuation of what has just transpired in Chapter 4 as you can see by the conjunction "but". This means there is going to be something that is in contrast to what has just been shared. Going all the way back to verse 32, it's relative to the early church practice of sharing things and having all things in common and taking care of one another. The reason they were doing this was because first, it identified Biblical fellowship. They were preoccupied with two things.

1. Taking care of each other and seeing that there was no need that would go unmet and,

2. They were a people on mission to propagate the gospel.

Their unity focused on those two matters. Quite honestly, there will always be unity if our priorities are the same—loving God and loving each other. God's love prompted them to passionately share their new found faith and their love for each other compelled them to give sacrificially, spontaneously and significantly.

It is in this context that we are introduced to Joseph, who was also known as Barnabas. He was known as the "son of encouragement". This man has always been one of my favorite Biblical characters. He's a gracious giver, disciple maker, motivated missionary, and peacemaker. He personifies what a sold-out, born again Christian looks like. He's the real deal. When I read about Barnabas I want to be like him. I want to build people up. I want to be an encourager and inspire people to love the Lord their God with all their heart, soul, mind and strength. I want to be a gracious giver. I often say that you can divide people into two groups—the givers and the takers. God's love is manifest in those who love to give and they're the ones who find joy in living.

A. An Act of Devotion

Barnabas had some oceanfront property on the island of Cyprus. Mary and I recently went on a Bible Land Cruise and stopped at that beautiful eastern Mediterranean Island and enjoyed the beauty of that magnificent destination. Undoubtedly, Barnabas' property would have been worth a sizeable amount of money. Regardless, we read that he brought the money "and laid it at the apostle's feet" (Acts 4:37). Out of a devoted and disciplined heart he gave it all.

There is an interesting phenomenon in giving. When God gets a person's heart, you don't have to plead with them to give. Their giving is spontaneous and it's an overflow of a devoted heart. Let me say this, if you are not currently tithing to your church, let me encourage and challenge you to begin today. If that appeal is offensive, then there undoubtedly is a deeper problem. God's promise about tithing is this—"Test Me in this way, says the LORD of hosts. See if I will not open the floodgates of heaven and pour out a blessing for you without measure" (Malachi 3:10). God blesses financial faithfulness.

B. An Act of Deception

We are introduced to a man named Ananias and his wife Sapphira. Not unlike Barnabas, they sold a piece of property. All I can say is this—it must have been a better real estate market than today! Instead of giving it all, though, they concealed some of it and were trying to double dip on the money—give their money and get the spiritual prestige and recognition, but also hoard some for themselves and enjoy the windfall.

Don't misunderstand—keeping some money for themselves was not the sin. Peter clearly states that in verse 4—we're not commanded anywhere to give everything (perhaps with the exception of the rich young ruler). The overt sin was lying—publicly pretending to give all of the proceeds of the sale. It was the hypocrisy of the lie that did them in. I had an Independent Baptist tell me "What happened to Ananias and Sapphira is what happens when you tithe on the NET instead of the GROSS!" But, I submit to you, it was a problem of pretentiousness. They wanted to be seen and applauded by their spiritual colleagues for their sacrificial giving, but they were only playing the game and God caught them in a big ole' lie.

God's church needs you to be faithful in your giving. God's word says to give in proportion as God has blessed you and the place God's word says you ought to give is where you worship. I promise you, we at Lenexa Baptist Church, will be good stewards of God's money.

II. A CONDEMNATION FROM GOD

Then Peter said, "Ananias, why has Satan filled your heart to lie to the Holy Spirit and keep back part of the proceeds from the field? Wasn't it yours while you possessed it? And after it was sold, wasn't it at your disposal? Why is it that you planned this thing in your heart? You have not lied to men but to God!" When he heard these words, Ananias dropped dead, and a great fear came on all who heard. The young men got up, wrapped his body, carried him out, and buried him. There was an interval of about three hours; then his wife came in, not knowing what had happened. "Tell me," Peter asked her, "did you sell the field for this price?" "Yes," she said, "for that price." Then Peter said to her, "Why did you agree to test the Spirit of the Lord? Look! The feet of those who have buried your husband are at the door, and they will carry you out!" Instantly she dropped dead at his feet. When the young men came in, they found her dead, carried her out, and buried her beside her husband." (Acts 5:3–10)

Who can argue, this punishment seems severe and over the top. But obviously hypocrisy and greed, pretentiousness and lying to the Holy Spirit are no small matters. I John 5 tells us there is a sin that leads to death. We see that here. It's happened in Scripture on a few occasions. It happened in Corinth for drunkenness and misbehavior at the Lord's Table. It happened in the Old Testament with Nadab and Abihu, the sons of Aaron and it certainly happened with Achan. The Bible declares there is a sin that leads to death.

A. Spiritual Perception

This deceit of Ananias and Sapphira didn't fool the Apostle Peter. He was guided by the Holy Spirit and saw through to their hypocrisy. You can only guess how stunned Ananias must have been. After all, he had been receiving "kudos" from everyone for his gift. Peter certainly brought it to an abrupt halt when he said, "Satan's influence has filled your heart to lie to the Holy Spirit." Still, while Satan was involved in tempting Ananias to keep and conceal his proceeds, it did not in any way lessen his personal responsibility for his actions. He had the freedom to choose what was right or to let the lie Satan had put before him lead him into darkness. He chose to take the low road.

I wonder….how well do you handle temptation? Do you keep your guard up against Satan, clothing yourself in the armor of God? Are you mature enough to put the brakes on when you sense your resistance is low? Here's the truth about sin. Whatever is done in darkness will be brought to light. We're all vulnerable, but praise

God "because greater is He who is in you, than he who is in the world" (I John 4:4, KJV). Oscar Wilde said, "I can resist anything but temptation."[11] I am reminded of the verse, "No temptation has overtaken you except what is common to humanity. God is faithful and He will not allow you to be tempted beyond what you are able, but with the temptation He will also provide a way of escape, so that you are able to bear it" (I Corinthians 10:13).

B. Serious Punishment

This punishment was swift and it was severe. God's judgment was rendered and suddenly Ananias was dead. He is whisked away by some able bodied young men who were standing close by. They took him to the closest cemetery and immediately gave him a customary burial, which in first century Israel was required to be the same day. Deuteronomy 21 gives the command that when divine judgment takes place, that person is to go to their grave that very day.

The second account in this melodrama takes place about three hours later when Sapphira came in having no idea that her husband was six feet under. Peter asked her the exploratory question, "Did you sell the property for this particular price?" She said, "Yes." Just like her husband, she lied and she died. The same pallbearers who had just returned from Ananias' burial spot took her and it was a twin killing and a twin burial. Why? Because of the hypocrisy and the fact that they lied to the Holy Spirit in an effort to get glory for themselves, while they had pretentiously deceived others, leading them to believe they had given their all.

Vance Havner, a Baptist pastor, now deceased wrote, "If God still dealt with people today as He did with Ananias and Sapphira, every church would have to have a morgue in the basement."[12] And who can argue? This punishment seems to exceed the crime. Why did God judge them so severely? Let me just say God does a lot of things that perplex me. While this punishment is severe and monumental, it could have been that God was destroying a body to save a soul. James 5:20 says, "he should know that whoever turns a sinner from the error of his way will save his life from death and cover a multitude of sins."

No doubt, some have wondered whether or not Ananias and Sapphira were true believers. I feel confident they were, first, because they were included in the congregation of believers. Conjecture is that they were saved on the Day of Pentecost when Peter preached and the Holy Spirit breathed new life into 3,000 Jews celebrating in Jerusalem. Second, they were involved with the Holy Spirit, giving indication that the Holy Spirit indwelt them from the time of their conversion. Anyone who hasn't been saved doesn't have God's Spirit possessing their life. Thirdly, God was using them as examples to the church of how disobedience and hypocrisy would not be tolerated. It would be an effective example for a significant time to come! God surgically removed them from His body, lest this infection destroy the newly founded church. They were the shameful examples of God's intolerance against hypocrisy

III. THE CONSEQUENCE OF GRIEF

Then great fear came on the whole church and on all who heard these things. (Acts 5:11)

This was the first act of church discipline and it was severe. The reason, however, that God's word commands church discipline is to deter others from sin. "Publicly rebuke those who sin, so that the rest will also be afraid" (I Timothy 5:20).

A. A Fearful Emotion

Twice we read here that great fear came upon them as they witnessed this judgment on Ananias and Sapphira. No doubt God was teaching the early church some critical lessons. One of the things that arrests our attention and solidifies our bond together is a common fear. While we're told in the Bible not to fear, it is referencing things or circumstances—not God. Proverbs tells us, "The fear of the LORD is the beginning of knowledge" (Proverbs 1:7).

Oswald Chambers, the great devotional writer said, "The remarkable thing about fearing God is that when you fear God, you fear nothing else, whereas, if you do not fear God, you fear everything else."[13] I recently read what people fear more than anything else is not crime, illness or even death, but the greatest fear is their own feelings of these three things:

- Loneliness
- Helplessness
- Insignificance

These are the three phobias people struggle to cope with. Isn't it interesting that all of these have their solution in Jesus Christ?

- To the lonely—"I am always with you; you hold me by my right hand" (Psalm 73:23, NIV). "…And remember, I am with you always, to the end of the age" (Matthew 28:20).
- To the helpless—"And my God will supply all your needs according to His riches in glory in Christ Jesus" (Phil. 4:19). "I am able to do all things through Him who strengthens me" (Phil. 4:13).
- To those living with no purpose—"For everything, absolutely everything….got started in Him and finds its purpose in Him" (Colossians 1:16, The Message). If your life seems insignificant, then know in Jesus your life will find its meaning.

In our text, this fear was well founded. God had shown Himself to be intolerant of hypocrisy and pretense.

B. Flourishing Expansion

Life continues on here in the aftermath of this deadly judgment with what transpired. God was at work. People were being saved and the Lord was adding to the church in increasing numbers. It obviously gave indication that this incident with Ananias and Sapphira, as drastic and dramatic as it was, resulted in the gospel going forth and people being saved and brought into the Kingdom. I guarantee you this—these early believers here had an uncompromising commitment to holiness and this holiness sprang out of right and reverent fear of a holy God.

Understand me on this—Ananias and Sapphira were losers because they lost out on how exciting things were becoming in the life of the early church to all the believers in and around Jerusalem. God was doing some incredible things and they missed out. You too can miss out on God's best if you live in hypocrisy and disobedience. While I wouldn't suggest that a fate so tragic as Ananias and Sapphira would be yours, I can be confident your life will always be in want if you live apart and independent of God's will.

So, in light of this twin tragedy, what lessons can we apply to our lives? I see two quick lessons here. First, I believe God is telling us to:

1. Give Faithfully

From Genesis to Revelation, God has called us to be giving people. It has always been an act of worship to give to our God. God commended Barnabas and condemned Ananias and Sapphira, and it was relative to rightful stewardship. God always has called his covenant people to give faithfully. It goes all the way back to Genesis 14, when Abraham encountered the Priest of Salem, Melchizedek, a clear typology of our High Priest, the Lord Jesus Christ. When Abraham met him he gave him one tenth of his possessions. Without a mandate, without the Levitical law which came 400 years later, he knew in his heart that giving to God was expected. The New Testament is saturated with giving mandates. One out of 5 verses in the New Testament speaks about our relationship to possessions or money. The Apostle Paul writes, "Remember this: the person who sows sparingly will also reap sparingly, and the person who sows generously will also reap generously. Each person should do as he has decided in his heart—not out of regret or out of necessity, for God loves a cheerful giver" (II Corinthians 9:6–7).

2. Live with Integrity

The incriminating catalyst for God's judgment was that Ananias and Sapphira lied, deceived, and played the fool and God severely and swiftly took them to their grave. What's the lesson? Integrity, honesty, and truthfulness are God's expectation and mandate for us.

If we want God's blessing and benefits, we must walk in righteousness and truth. Integrity is who we are when no one is looking. Integrity should be the calling card for all of us who know the Lord Jesus.

Chapter Seven

The Priests, The Punishment and The Prohibition

Leviticus 10:1–11

I. THEIR PRIESTLY CALLING

A. The Family

B. The Function

II. THEIR PERSONAL CORRUPTION

A. The Offering

B. The Offense

III. THE PROBABLE CAUSE

As we saw in the last chapter—losers sometimes come in pairs. It was true in the New Testament with Ananias and Sapphira and we see it true in the Old Testament as well with two brothers named Nadab and Abihu. This obscure and obstinate duo take their place among our growing list of loser's as they broke the commands of God and paid the consequences with the death penalty. It seems when God comes in judgment, the death penalty is enacted without appeal to any governor or higher court. His judgments are swift and severe.

This week in Missouri, the execution of Roderick Nunley was cancelled. Nunley kidnapped, raped and murdered a 15 year old girl from Kansas City 21 years ago, but he has yet to be executed. After asking for a judge to sentence him, the judge did and gave him the death penalty. Now his appeal is that a judge doesn't have the authority to order a death sentence. So, 21 years have passed and still there remains a stay of execution. But when God comes in judgment, as here in our text, it is swift and it is severe. We see this once again in God's word.

I. THEIR PRIESTLY CALLING

Aaron's sons Nadab and Abihu each took his own firepan, put fire in it, placed incense on it, and presented unauthorized fire before the LORD, which He had not commanded them to do. (Leviticus 10:1)

In the book of Leviticus, we learn about the establishment of the Israelite's sacrificial system and the role that the priests would play in this elaborate plan of God. Actually, Leviticus 9 ends on a spiritual affirmation of Jehovah on the sacrificial system as God sent fire down from heaven consuming the burnt offering that Aaron had prepared and the people shouted and fell on their faces before the Lord. Now when we come to Chapter 10, we are introduced to two of Aaron's sons—his firstborn named Nadab and his second born, Abihu.

A. Their Family

Nadab and Abihu were born into a prestigious family. Their father was Aaron and their uncle was Moses. You remember Aaron was called by God to be Moses' spokesman and his assistant. But also God's specific calling to Aaron was to be the first priest. He would be responsible to directly receive God's message and then relay that message to the people. That's what a priest would do. They were the "go-betweens" who had the responsibility of offering the sacrifices at the altar on behalf of God's people. The Hebrew word for priest is "Kohen" and is used 775 times in the Old Testament. The original high priest was Aaron and, in that Nadab and Abihu were his sons, they were also set apart by God to hold this esteemed and treasured position. The age of entering the priesthood was between 25-30 years old, and while we're uncertain of Nadab and Abihu's ages, we know that Nadab left no descendants according to Numbers chapter 3. So these brothers had a calling of God on their lives and it was a high and holy calling.

Honestly, it's true for all of us in this dispensation, who God has saved. We have the calling of God on our lives. God's desire in the Old Testament, according to Exodus 19, is to have His people become a kingdom of priests. But their sinful and rebellious ways prohibited it. But now in New Testament times, the Apostle Peter writes that we, as believers in Jesus Christ, are a chosen people, a royal priesthood, a holy nation, a people for His possession so that we may proclaim His praises. This New Testament doctrine that we as Baptists treasure is called the Priesthood of the Believer. It means we no longer need a priest as our go-between because when Christ died on Calvary for our sins, the veil was torn and now the honor and privilege of entering the Holy of Holies (which was reserved for only the High Priest) is available to everyone who has trusted in Jesus Christ, who is our High Priest. "Seeing then that we have a great High Priest who has passed through the heavens, Jesus the Son of God, let us hold fast our confession. For we do not have a High Priest who cannot sympathize with our weaknesses, but was in all points tempted as we are, yet without sin. Let us therefore come boldly to the throne of grace, that we may obtain mercy and find grace to help in time of need" (Hebrews 4:14–16, NKJV).

So, do you understand why we as Protestants don't have priests? Because the Bible says we don't need them any longer. "For there is one God and one mediator between God and men, the man Christ Jesus" (I Timothy 2:5, NKJV). We go directly to God in prayer to confess our sins. This is because our high priest, the Lord Jesus, offered the final and greatest sacrifice—Himself, the Lamb of God who has taken away the sins of the world.

B. The Function

According to Numbers 16:5, the priestly office that was established by Aaron and his descendants had three elements:

1. They were chosen by God—

The priests were to be from the tribe of Levi and the High Priest was to come from the line of Aaron. Then the priests were set apart for service to Jehovah.

2. They had to be holy—

This meant, first, that they were set apart, but they also were to be consecrated and holy before God. King David asked in his Psalm, "who can come into your Holy hill?" His answer in the next verse is, "He who has clean hands and a pure heart, who has not lifted up his soul to an idol, nor sworn deceitfully" (Psalm 24:4, NKJV).

3. They were allowed to come near to God—

So, while the people had no authority or right and certainly no personal righteousness to come into God's presence, it was not so with a priest. God had ordained them for their calling.

So, the priests would attend to things in the tabernacle; the changing of the showbread in the Holy place and what we see in the text—the burning of incense. Still only the High Priest could enter into the Holy of Holies. He entered one time a year on Yom Kipper to offer a blood sacrifice for the sins of the people by sprinkling the blood of the sacrificial goat on the mercy seat. But after Christ came, all that changed. "He entered the Holy of Holies once for all, not by the blood of goats and calves, but by His own blood, having obtained eternal redemption" (Hebrews 9:12). So Jesus became our High Priest that we might all become a kingdom of priests. But as God expected holiness and purity, faithfulness and charity among His priests, so He expects the same from us today.

II. THEIR PERSONAL CORRUPTION

Then flames leaped from the LORD's presence and burned them to death before the LORD. So Moses said to Aaron, "This is what the LORD meant when He said: I will show My holiness to those who are near Me, and I will reveal My glory before all the people." But Aaron remained silent. Moses summoned Mishael and Elzaphan, sons of Aaron's uncle Uzziel, and said to them. "Come here and carry your relatives away from the front of the sanctuary to a place outside the camp." So they came forward and carried them in their tunics outside the camp, as Moses had said. Then Moses said to Aaron and his sons Eleazar and Ithamar, "Do not let your hair hang loose and do not tear your garments, or else you will die, and the LORD will become angry with the whole community. However, your brothers, the whole house of Israel, may mourn over that tragedy when the LORD sent the fire. You must not go outside the entrance to the tent of meeting or you will die, for the LORD's anointing oil is on you." So they did as Moses said". (Leviticus 10:2–7)

Nadab and Abihu were beginning their priestly ministry on the first official day of operation and suffice it to say things got off to a bad start. I've heard of people getting fired their first day on the job, but that literally happened with these two irreverent rebels.

A. Their Offering

Moses, who is the author of the Pentateuch, tells us here that Nadab and Abihu took censers and put fire in them and added incense to them. According to the text described here in Leviticus and Exodus, the priests were to burn incense on the brazen altar, both morning and evening. So burning this incense was an expectation along with trimming the wicks on the lamp stand, lighting the menorah and putting showbread on the table of presence every Sabbath. However, something went sorely wrong here. As the text said, they offered strange or profane fire (unauthorized fire) and obviously they didn't follow the Lord's command.

B. Their Offense

This profane or strange fire offered here has been debated by Biblical commentators over the centuries. Actually, the Jewish rabbis proposed 12 theories to explain the death of Nadab and Abihu. Let's look at the three most common solutions to this judgment by God. First, they went too far into the temple area and went past the veil into the Holy of Holies, which has a strong Biblical argument because in Leviticus 17, the sin of Nadab and Abihu is being discussed when Aaron is being warned not to enter into the

Holy of Holies except on the Day of Atonement. Second, some believe it was fire from unauthorized coals from outside the temple area, thus it was profane. The third argument was the incense didn't contain the proper ingredients, which was a legitimate argument since the problem seems to be with the nature of the fire itself. The commentator suggested strange fire implied it was fire kindled for the purpose of worshipping other deities. As it says in verse 1, it was contrary to God's command—which is used in context of worshipping other pagan deities.

What we do know about this offense is that it was a deadly offense, as God sent down fire from heaven. Actually, twelve times in the Old Testament we find God sending down fire from heaven. Six times it's in a beneficial way, like Elijah at Mt. Carmel. The other six times—as it is here—it is in judgment and surely we declare here in our text with the writer of Hebrews, our God is a consuming fire.

Here's the application for us today. God takes seriously how we handle worship. He seems to be intolerant of presumption, disobedience and even carelessness. The tendency of most 21st century Christians is that we're too cavalier about God's commands.

In Exodus 19, God had warned the priests that judgment would be inevitable if they were disobedient in their offerings to Him. But Nadab and Abihu thought that commandment was for everybody else and that's what happens to many believers today. Oh, people agree that honesty and integrity are expected and mandated by God but when coloring outside the lines of honesty seems to benefit them, then that law is for everybody else. Have you ever known anyone who thought the law was for everybody else but them? It's chronic among celebrities. That's why Paris Hilton or Lindsey Lohan seem appalled when they have to go to jail for a DUI or for possession of drugs. But this way of thinking is common among believers as well. I've seen many Christians who thought this matter of financial giving that God commands is for someone else or that prioritizing worship and faithfulness in God's house over competitive sports or recreational activities is for others. Presumptuously they say, "Oh, God will understand". But I would say to you, while He is longsuffering, He still is intolerant of disobedience. Understand, all the commands and all the laws in this Bible are for me and for you.

In our text when Nadab and Abihu died, their uncles, Mishael and Elzaphan, were commissioned by Moses to remove their bodies from the Tabernacle. The other priests would have been marked unclean by touching a dead person. God then told Aaron and the other brethren not to mourn. Aaron was silent….this was quite a contrast to what usually happened when someone died in the Ancient Near East. There was usually wailing and lamenting and tearing their clothes. But God said, "We'll have none of that" and the grief and sorrow of Aaron's family would have to be contained.

III. THE PROBABLE CAUSE

The LORD spoke to Aaron: "You and your sons are not to drink wine or beer when you enter the tent of meeting, or else you will die: This is a permanent statute throughout your generations. You must distinguish between the holy and the common, and the clean and the unclean, and teach the Israelites all the statutes that the LORD has given to them through Moses." (Leviticus 10:8–11)

What is it that prompts people to this kind of blatant disobedience? Had Nadab and Abihu simply forgotten or ignored the clear commands from Jehovah regarding what they were to do and what they were not to do?

I think we get a window into their deadly sin right here in the context. As you know, one of the first principles to interpret scripture is to look at the context. Right after the deaths of Aaron's sons, God tells him, "Don't come into my tabernacle intoxicated. Not you or your sons, or else what happened to Nadab and Abihu will happen to Eleazar and Ithamar or anyone else who staggers into my house drunk." So it seems to me Nadab and Abihu, the fateful day of their death, had been up early drinking and losing their inhibitions about their first day on the job as priests of God. The cause of their irreverent behavior can be traced back to hard liquor. Proverbs 31 teaches, "it is not for kings to drink wine….otherwise, they will drink, forget what is decreed, and pervert justice" (Proverbs 31:4–5).

In the New Testament, the church leaders, elders and deacons are commanded to be men who are not given to wine. Why? It's because alcohol dulls the mind. It subdues inhibitions and under the influence, people who are otherwise sensible and subdued get out of control and behave in a way they otherwise never would. That's what alcohol will do. 43% of Americans are dealing with alcoholism in their families. 17,488 people died last year in alcohol related deaths. I'm simply telling you that alcohol will make losers out of any winners. Nadab and Abihu were born into a privileged position—the tribe of Levi and sons of Aaron. Their irresponsibility and intoxication made them behave in a way that cost them their lives. That's the all too often storyline of alcohol.

I close with this sad personal story. I am the only survivor in my immediate family. My mom and dad are both deceased and my sister, Susan, died of alcoholism at 49 years of age. But also, I had a cousin who my parents adopted when I was 7 years old. His name was Royce. He was 14 years old when he moved in with us after his mother's death. So, suddenly, I had an older brother and I looked up to him a lot because I loved sports and he was a gifted athlete. We had a close brother-like relationship. We fought like brothers and we loved each other like brothers. Royce graduated from High School as an all-state running back, was the MVP in the Oil Bowl, state champion in the 100 yard dash, and state champion in the pole vault. He was recruited by several division one schools to play football, but he signed with the University of Oklahoma to run track.

But as with so many, he started drinking, his drinking led to irresponsibility, and pretty soon alcohol had its claws deep into the fiber of his being. It was so bad he had to leave the states and move to Germany. He coached football and worked in a civilian job there, but his alcohol issues got him run out of Germany. He moved to Panama and was finally able to return to the states. He went through AA and was sober for a season, but fell off the wagon. His life became so pitiful that I'm ashamed to share it. I will never forget that day. It was on Saturday, May 6th, 1995 that we were having a work day over at our church on Bourgade. I was working in the flower beds when Mary pulled into the parking lot. I went to the window of her car and she said, "Steve, your mom just called and Royce is dead. He shot himself in his apartment in Denton, TX." My heart sank and I put my face in my hands and I cried and cried. I returned to Ada to do his funeral, and while I gave him a eulogy that capsulated his life, I concluded by saying, "Let's be honest. Alcohol, not a pistol, took Royce's life." And it had.

We see the same storyline in a Biblical story that took place 3500 years ago. It was the undoing of Nadab and Abihu and it will be your undoing as well. This series is about learning life's lessons from life's losers. Let's learn today the shameful lesson and not let alcohol ruin our lives.

Chapter Eight

A Wicked Wife and Her Wicked Ways

I Kings 16:31

I. A DOMINEERING DIVA
- A. Her Background
- B. Her Beauty
- C. Her Belief

II. A DEVILISH DEED
- A. Selfishness of Ahab
- B. Scheme of Jezebel
- C. Sentence of Elijah

III. A DETERMINED DESTINY

If there is one bad girl of the Bible that seems to personify evil, licentiousness and lewdness it is Jezebel, the one-time queen of Israel. While she lived nearly 3,000 years ago, still the spirit and the legend of the rebellious renegade lives on in infamy today because Jezebel is often identified with wickedness and even witchcraft. Some would argue that it's the spirit of Jezebel that birthed feminism—that growing sentiment to emasculate all men, rid them of their authority; and all the while fostering a hatred of men in general. For Jezebel not only ran roughshod over her husband, but also over God's prophet and anyone else who would get in her way. No doubt Jezebel mocked

God and manipulated her husband to maneuver her way into power and prominence. She was a deceiver, a destroyer, and a deranged defrauder. Nevertheless, we can learn many positive truths from her negative and naughty life.

Jezebel is mentioned over 20 times in the Bible. She's even mentioned in the New Testament in the book of Revelation as the Apostle John wrote to the church of Thyatira and condemned them for their tolerance of evil. God identified a woman named Jezebel who led this Asian church in idolatry and sexual immorality. This reference to Jezebel undoubtedly was a nickname given to this woman who infected this church with her promiscuousness and paganism.

I. A DOMINEERING DIVA

Still there was no one like Ahab, who devoted himself to do what was evil in the LORD'S sight, because his wife Jezebel incited him." (I Kings 21:25)

We are introduced to Jezebel in the historical book of I Kings. Actually, I and II Kings are part of a larger part of the Old Testament known as the 12 historical books; Joshua through Esther. In I Kings, we find what you would expect—the history of the kings and the kingdoms of Israel, also known as the Northern Kingdom, and Judah, also known as the Southern Kingdom. This is where we are introduced to what I'm calling a Domineering Diva and it's a fitting title for this daring and reckless yet influential woman who was married to King Ahab.

A. Her Background

Jezebel was the daughter of Ethbaal, King of Sidon. Her father was not only King but also a priest of Baal. She was born into a family of pagan idolatry. I doubt if I can overstate how significant this was as she would come and bring her pagan and perverted practices to Israel. Her husband, Ahab, was arguably one of the most evil Kings of Israel. Being the Domineering Diva that she was, Jezebel did her part in leading him away from Jehovah into his own practice of idolatry. Actually, it was so prevalent that Ahab built a magnificent temple in Samaria to the worship of Baal, Ashtareth and Astarte. Jezebel then erected a sanctuary for the priests of Baal where she fed 400 of them at her own table. Suffice it to say, Jezebel was a strong and domineering woman who got her way by taking her husband by the hand and leading him into darkness and deplorable idolatry.

Let me just say parenthetically here—women are tremendous influencers. While we've heard it said, "It's a man's world", I'm not so sure that is accurate anymore. I'm told women now control 70% of the world's wealth, which is not that surprising to me since a woman controls 100% of the wealth at my house!

So Jezebel was not only the daughter of a King but also a King's wife. She was used to having things her own way. She may have had the secondary position in the palace, but just like Hillary ran the White House, so Jezebel ruled the throne of Israel.

B. Her Beauty

Jezebel's reputation was one of being evil and heartless, yet she also was known to be a lady who turned heads because of her outward adornment. Herbert Lockyer writes, "When Ahab laid eyes on her, he was fascinated by her beauty and the forcefulness of her character and he fell for her. Jezebel seized the opportunity to rule the nation of Israel."[14] But Jezebel is the personification of the phrase "Beauty is only skin deep". Actually, the name Jezebel means "chaste, free from carnal connection". This surely must have been the desire of her parents as they named their baby girl. For Jezebel, though, no name could have been more inappropriate for she was anything but chaste and free from carnality because this was the avenue where she lived. Dr. R.G. Lee wrote of Jezebel in his famous sermon, Payday Someday—"She was as blatant in her wickedness and as brazen in her lewdness as was Cleopatra of Egypt and she had the adulterous desire rivaled only by Potiphar's wife."[15]

A. Her Belief

Jezebel was a devout worshipper of Baal. She hated anyone and everyone who spoke against or refused to worship at her pagan altars. This zeal for Baal thus led to the ensuing and infamous battle of Elijah the prophet with the prophets of Baal in I Kings 18.

Baal worship was the common pagan worship in Canaan, Phoenicia and Mesopotamia. Baal worship involved the worship of the god Dagan who was associated with agriculture. The belief was that this false god gave the increase to farmers in the fields and was responsible for the increase of their flocks and herds. Another god associated with Baal worship was the god Hadad, whose voice was believed to be heard in the thunder and accompanying rain. So when Elijah predicted a drought and there was no rainfall it fueled the anger of this brash and bigoted Jezebel. After Elijah defeated her pagan prophets on Carmel, she put out the decree for God's prophet to be slaughtered just like the 450 prophets of Baal had been slaughtered on Carmel by Elijah.

Baal worship was more than the worship of Dagan and Hadad. It was more than bowing down to an agricultural deity or storm god. It was also licentious and sexual. You would find in their high places of worship chambers reserved for both male and female prostitutes. Part of their perverted worship was to be involved in orgies and all kinds of sexual perversions. It is easy to see how the Israelites were often drawn away from Jehovah who mandated personal holiness and sexual purity. These pagan deities of Baal appealed to their sexual and lustful carnal appetite. This was Jezebel's religion and her pagan and profane worship led her into darker and more despicable exploitations.

II. A DEVELISH DEED

In I Kings 21, we find just how devilish and depraved Jezebel really was. This is the narrative of Naboth's vineyard. Naboth was a devout Israelite who lived close to King Ahab's summer palace in the town of Jezreel, where he owned a little vineyard. Ahab's edifice was an impressive palace in that it was inlaid with ivory, the first ever constructed. What a contrast to the meager little vineyard that Naboth had inherited from his ancestors. But as is always the case, money and material possessions never satisfy, they always leave us wanting more. So it was with this wicked king.

A. Selfishness of Ahab

So Ahab spoke to Naboth, saying "Give me your vineyard so I can have it for a vegetable garden, since it is right next to my palace. I will give you a better vineyard in its place, or if you prefer, I will give you its value in silver."But Naboth said to Ahab, "I will never give my fathers' inheritance to you." So Ahab went to his palace resentful and angry, because of what Naboth the Jezreelite had told him. He had said, "I will not give you my fathers' inheritance." He lay down on his bed, turned his face away, and didn't eat any food. (I Kings 21:2–4)

With Ahab, it's a classic case of covetousness. He wanted what Naboth had and because it was a treasured family inheritance, Naboth wasn't interested in the King's offer. So we see Ahab return home and begin to pout like a spoiled child because his offer had been rejected by Naboth. The king who lived in the lap of luxury with ivory, gold and precious stones at his disposal was now acting like a blubbering baby because he didn't get what he wanted, a little vegetable garden, and he was ill with envy. Envy has been called the sickness that will not go away; the most corroding of vices and it was certainly true with Ahab. As we see, his selfishness led to action on Jezebel's part.

B. Scheme of Jezebel

Then his wife Jezebel came to him and said to him, "Why are you so upset that you refuse to eat?" "Because I spoke to Naboth the Jezreelite," he replied. "I told him: Give me your vineyard for silver, or if you wish, I will give you a vineyard in its place." But he said, "I won't give you my vineyard!" Then his wife Jezebel said to him, "Now, exercise your royal power over Israel. Get up, eat some food, and be happy. For I will give you the vineyard of Naboth the Jezreelite." So she wrote letters in Ahab's name and sealed them with his seal. She sent the letters to the elders and nobles who lived with Naboth in his city. In the letters, she wrote: Proclaim a fast and seat Naboth at the head of the people. Then seat two wicked men opposite him and have them testify against him, saying, 'You have cursed God and king!' Then take him out and stone him to death. The men of his city, the elders and nobles who lived in his city, did as Jezebel had commanded them, as was written in the letters she had sent them. They proclaimed a fast and seated Naboth at the head of the people. The two wicked men came in and sat opposite him. Then the wicked men testified against Naboth in the presence of the people, saying, "Naboth has cursed God and king!" So they took him outside the city and stoned him to death with stones. Then they sent word to Jezebel, "Naboth has been stoned to death." When Jezebel heard that Naboth had been stoned to death, she said to Ahab, "Get up and take possession of the vineyard of Naboth the Jezreelite who refused to give it to you for silver, since Naboth isn't alive, but dead." When Ahab heard that Naboth was dead, he got up to go down to the vineyard of Naboth the Jezreelite to take possession of it. (I Kings 21:5–16)

Naboth's pouting prompted Jezebel to action and first she says, "Look…exercise your power. Doesn't Naboth know who he's messing with? And by the way," shouted Jezebel, "Did you forget you're the king?" As you would expect from her, she takes over and declares, "I'll get that vineyard from that meager, measly, miser! Who does he thing he is?"

So we see the plot was to proclaim a fast and invite the city officials and to hire two hit men. Jezebel concocts this scheme and then in the presence of the dignitaries, Naboth is accused of treason and blasphemy. They take him outside the city and stone him to death. This cruel and barbaric method of execution was reserved for those who practiced idolatry, seduced others, or committed blasphemy. All that Naboth was guilty of was getting in the way of an evil woman who had no regard for anybody or anything that stood in her way. This devilish deed captures and communicates this evil lady that now lives in infamy.

In spite of this the name of Jezebel has taken on a kind of cult following in the 21st century with Jezebel magazine, Jezebel lingerie, Jezebel on Twitter, and Jezebel.com. It seems this worldly, beguiling, lewd and murderous woman has carnal appeal. While she lines up today in this growing list of losers, I can only conclude there are many out there who want to identify with her in her devilish deceit. But here's what I know—the pleasures of sin are but for a season. There was a payday coming for it is written in God's constitution to everyone. "And as it is appointed unto men once to die, and after this the judgment:" (Hebrews 9:27, KJV). This wicked and worldly woman too, would face God's judgment, but, so it will be for all who go the way of Jezebel, who choose to live in sin and ignore the ways of our God. I doubt if anyone of you would be so twisted and vile as this corrupt queen, but the Bible declares, "As it is written: There is no one righteous, not even one;…For all have sinned and fall short of the glory of God (Romans 3: 10, 23) and "For the wages of sin is death, but the gift of God is eternal life in Christ Jesus our Lord" (Romans 6:23). Just as Jezebel would soon seal her fate so will you if you neglect so great a salvation. Jesus said there is a broad road that leads to destruction and many are on that path.

C. Sentence of Elijah

Then the word of the LORD came to Elijah the Tishbite: "Get up and go to meet Ahab king of Israel, who is in Samaria. You'll find him in Naboth's vineyard, where he has gone to take possession of it. Tell him, "This is what the LORD says: Have you murdered and also taken possession?" Then tell him, "This is what the LORD says: In the place where the dogs licked Naboth's blood, the dogs will also lick your blood!" Ahab said to Elijah, "So, you have caught me, my enemy." He replied, "I have caught you because you devoted yourself to do what is evil in the LORD'S sight. This is what the LORD says: "I am about to bring disaster on you and will sweep away your descendants: I will eliminate all of Ahab's males, both slave and free, in Israel; I will make your house like the house of Jeroboam son of Nebat and like the house of Baasha son of Ahijah, because you have provoked My anger and caused Israel to sin. The LORD also speaks of Jezebel: The dogs will eat Jezebel in the plot of land at Jezreel:" (I Kings 21:17–23)

Suddenly, in verse 20, Elijah the prophet reappears after not being heard of for awhile. You remember this brave prophet who defeated the prophets of Baal on Mt. Carmel shockingly fled in fear from Jezebel who threatened his life. But that threat now has boomeranged and is coming back to Jezebel. It's just like God promises in His law of sowing and reaping, "Don't be deceived: God is not mocked. For whatever a man sows he will also reap," (Galatians 6:7).

If you finish reading this chapter in I Kings you will see that Ahab seemingly repented and God postponed his judgment. But the prophecy of the dogs licking up his blood would surely be fulfilled when the dogs licked up his blood as one of his servants washed out his chariot after the battle that cost him his life. And so also it was with Jezebel. The hammer of justice was about to fall and the hungry, scavenging dogs in Jezreel were about to feast on this loser from Phoenicia.

III. A DETERMINED DESTINY

When Jehu came to Jezreel, Jezebel heard about it, so she painted her eyes, adorned her head, and looked down from the window. As Jehu entered the gate, she said, "Do you come in peace, Zimri, killer of your master?" He looked up toward the window and said, "Who is on my side? Who?" Two or three eunuchs looked down at him, and he said, "Throw her down!" So they threw her down, and some of her blood splattered on the wall and on the horses, and Jehu rode over her. Then he went in, ate and drank, and said, "Take care of this cursed woman and bury her, since she's a king's daughter." But when they went out to bury her, they did not find anything but her skull, her feet, and the palms of her hands. So they went back and told him, and he said, "This fulfills the LORD'S word that He spoke through His servant Elijah the Tishbite: "In the plot of land at Jezreel, the dogs will eat Jezebel's flesh. Jezebel's corpse will be like manure on the surface of the field in the plot of land at Jezreel so that no one will be able to say: This is Jezebel." (II Kings 9:30–37)

After the death of Ahab, Jehu was to be anointed King by Elijah but for some reason Elijah didn't anoint him. Instead, his predecessor, Elisha, sent a message that Jehu was to be King of Israel and he was to destroy the house of Ahab. So Jehu took over the throne and in II Kings chapter 9, after slaughtering Joram, the son of Ahab, he threw Joram's body in the very vineyard belonging to Naboth. This fulfilled one of the prophetic judgments from Elijah.

The remaining prophecy regarding Jezreel was about to transpire and we pick up our story in II Kings. Jezebel, who had sown to the wind—idolatry, licentiousness, lewdness and vanity—now, had to reap a whirlwind of consequences and God's judgment was unavoidable. Here's what I want you to understand, from the time Elijah promised judgment on Ahab and Jezebel, there was about a three year time lag. They undoubtedly sat at their table enjoying the produce from what once was Naboth's little vineyard and perhaps they even joked about what Elijah had threatened and even sneered at his prophetic words. "Here Ahab enjoy these herbs and vegetables. You know, I thought the prophet said dogs were coming to lick up our blood. I guess they lost our scent," they chuckled together. But in the distance, there was a dog barking and in their soul they surely thought, "Could it be? Will it be? Is today the day? Oh no, surely not." But soon the seeds of wickedness began to sprout and the promise of God's prophet would soon be realized and with a made up face and a hardened heart, she was thrown to her death. The dogs destroyed and desecrated the corpse of this provocative princess, leaving only her skull, feet, and the palms of her hands.

In application of the life of Jezebel, three timeless truths are evident:

1. **Marrying outside the faith has serious implications.**

God had commanded His people not to intermarry with people outside of His covenant relationship. They were surrounded by pagan nations and the worship of Baal was prevalent in places like Canaan and Phoenicia, which was Jezebel's home. Sure enough, Ahab's faltering faith was soon engulfed by Jezebel's persistence and perversions and he too bowed down to the Baals.

God's word declares we're not to be unequally yoked with an unbeliever and I submit to you, there is nothing more important in marriage than a person's belief system. It's where we derive our core values. Marriages are often vulnerable and fragile, even among believers but with a common devotion to God, there is hope and resolve.

2. **Wrong worship results in wicked behavior.**

Jezebel was a devout worshipper of Baal, as was her father and grandfather. But her worship was pagan, promiscuous and profane. In this worship she saw people as disposable. Instead of valuing life, her irreverent idolatry resulted in murder, scandal and anarchy. You see, the problem is this, we become like what we worship. Kids want to be like the athlete they admire, or the rock star they listen to or a teacher they respect. Honestly, when we worship our God who is holy and just, loving and forgiving, we become more like Him.

3. **The promise of God's judgment will eventually be realized.**

We have seen in the last two chapters with Nadab and Abihu and Ananias and Sapphira that God's judgment was swift and severe. Instantaneously they were gone. But not so with Ahab or Jezebel; time elapsed before judgment came—three years in fact. But while it was delayed, it wasn't postponed indefinitely. There was to be a payday someday.

The wonderful truth of knowing Jesus Christ is this—He is the atoning sacrifice for our sins. The judgment for all of our sin, shame and hypocrisy falls upon Him when we place our trust in Him. God's word tells us, "He made the One who did not know sin to be sin for us, so that we might become the righteousness of God in Him" (II Corinthians 5:21) and "Therefore, no condemnation now exists for those in Christ Jesus" (Romans 8:1).

Chapter Nine

A Covert Conspiracy

Matthew 14:1–13

I. THE CORRUPTED MARRIAGE
   A. The Unlawful Conduct
   B. The Undoing Confrontation

II. THE COLLABORATED MURDER
   A. The Setting
   B. The Seduction
   C. The Shame

III. THE CONCURING MOURNING
   A. The Burial
   B. The Brokenness

In this study of Life's Lessons from Life's Losers, we have been on a quest to learn how we can avoid being labeled a loser. We've looked at a variety of personalities in these last eight chapters—men and women, two brothers, husbands and wives. The common denominator of all these people has been their personal compromise and their shameful disobedience to God. Without exception, their bad and detestable choices have cost them dearly.

One thing we know collectively is this; we are all losers, because who among us hasn't made wrong choices, mistakes and acted unwisely? But what ultimately makes us a loser is this; it's when our mistakes don't lead us back to God. It is only by the transforming power of Jesus Christ that a loser can instantly be made a winner. In Jesus old things are passed away and all things have become new.

Here's what I know about declaring a winner. It is done at the conclusion of the competition. I'll never forget the playoff game in January of 1993 between the Houston Oilers and the Buffalo Bills. I was actually travelling to Houston that Sunday afternoon with several preachers from Kansas City, to attend a Home Mission Board conference. Buffalo was behind 28–3 at half-time and in the 3rd quarter they were behind by 32 points. But with their backup quarterback Frank Reich leading the Bills, they came back to win the game in overtime 41–38. It was the largest comeback in NFL history. My point is this—winners are not declared until the end. That's the good news of the gospel of the Lord Jesus. It's never too late to change the outcome of your life because Jesus offers grace and forgiveness for every loser.

We are back in the New Testament now and are looking again at another woman. The last woman we considered was Jezebel, who ranks at the pinnacle of lady losers, but now we will look at a close second as we examine the life of Herodias. John MacArthur writes of Herodias, "She is one of the most wicked and perverse women mentioned in the Word of God, perhaps only rivaled by Jezebel."[16] So now we will consider Herodias, the Hasmonean heretic, who in a covert conspiracy killed the greatest man ever born of woman, John the Baptist.

I. THE CORRUPTED MARRIAGE

At that time Herod the tetrarch heard the report about Jesus. "This is John the Baptist!" he told his servants. "He has been raised from the dead, and that's why supernatural powers are at work in him." For Herod had arrested John, chained him, and put him in prison on account of Herodias, his brother Philip's wife, since John had been telling him, "It's not lawful for you to have her!" Though he wanted to kill him, he feared the crowd, since they regarded him as a prophet. (Matthew 14:1–5)

As chapter 14 begins, we are introduced to Herod, the tetrarch. He was the ruler in Israel who was the son of Herod the Great. We know him as Herod Antipas. When his father, Herod the Great died, the kingdom of Palestine was divided among three of the sons, Archaleus, Phillip and Antipas. Herod Antipas ruled the region between Galilee and Perea for several decades. We learn here that Herod Antipas, when he heard about the miracles and the magnetism of Jesus, thought that he might be John the Baptist reincarnated. Herod's guilt was seemingly haunting him and he was fearful that the mighty prophet of God was back. He knew he would be in trouble if that were true.

A. The Unlawful Conduct

Matthew, in verse 3, now begins to give the background for John's execution. Herod had John thrown into prison because of his outspoken condemnation of his marriage to our featured loser, Herodias. Herodias, you see, was once married to Phillip, the half brother of Herod Antipas. While Herodias and Phillip were estranged from each other, according to Roman law, the marriage was still unlawful. Plus, it was incestuous because Herodias was the daughter of Aristobulus, who was Herod Antipas' half brother. So Herod was not just marrying his brother's ex-wife he was also marrying his niece. Can you say dysfunctional? In the United States there are 25 states that prohibit marrying your first cousin. Still 6 states permit first cousins to marry under certain circumstances, which is either being over 65 or at least one of the partners is unable to reproduce. So suffice it to say, the marriage of Herodias was unlawful and incestuous. God's prophet, John the Baptist, would not shrink back from confronting this Galilean ruler.

B. The Undoing Confrontation

We have no record of where or how John had first confronted Herod about his unlawful marriage, but according to Mark's gospel, it seemed to have been on more than on one occasion. It seems that both Herod and Herodias were incensed and outraged at the prophet's presumption of telling them what was unacceptable. It seems they both desired to execute John, but obviously; it was more the desire of Herodias than of Antipas. His reluctance was relative to what the multitudes thought; that being, that John was a prophet. Killing a prophet would definitely not endear him to the multitudes. Here is what we learn about the baptizer; he was a man who would not compromise, nor was he a diplomat, for he wore the cloak of a prophet well.

In Matthew chapter 3 John was preaching in the wilderness of Judea and the text says many Pharisees and Sadducees came requesting baptism. "Brood of vipers! Who warned you to flee from the coming wrath? Therefore produce fruit consistent with repentance" (Matthew 3:7b–8). John is saying do this or else I'll not baptize any of you. I ask you; is that the best church growth strategy? It's not seeker friendly for sure! Honestly, it's the polar opposite of what is often being propagated in the pulpits across this country as many preachers poll the people to see what they want to hear rather than having a word from God that might bring conviction and discomfort. Here's what I want to know; what has happened to all the Elijah's, John the Baptists, the Billy Sunday's and the Adrian Rogers?

I'll never forget the story of what happened with Dr. Rogers, President of the Southern Baptist Convention, when he went to the White House upon invitation from President Jimmy Carter in 1979 and met with him in the Oval Office. Instead of playing the game of kissing up to the President, Dr. Rogers looked at him and said, "Mr. President, why do you call yourself a Southern Baptist when you're not. I hope you will give up your secular humanism and return to Christianity."[17] Suffice it to say, Dr. Rogers wasn't invited back to the White House! Fortunately, his confrontation was effective because we finally did get a resignation from Carter and now, praise God, he no longer calls himself a Southern Baptist.

II. THE COLLABORATED MURDER

But when Herod's birthday celebration came, Herodias' daughter danced before them and pleased Herod. So he promised with an oath to give her whatever she might ask. And prompted by her mother, she answered, "Give me John the Baptist's head here on a platter!" Although the king regretted it, he commanded that it be granted because of his oaths and his guests. So he sent orders and had John beheaded in the prison. His head was brought on a platter and given to the girl, who carried it to her mother. (Matthew 14:6–11)

As I mentioned, both Herod and Herodias wanted John dead. But Herod seemed to be content to leave him locked up in prison. Not so with his wicked wife so she, in a covert conspiracy, formulated a scheme to murder John.

A. The Setting

It was the celebration of Herod's birthday that was the occasion that Herodias unveiled her plot. The birthday party was definitely not a cake, punch, and pin the tail on the donkey affair. Rest assured it was pagan and provocative. Roman nobles were notorious for these stag birthday parties where gluttony, excessive drinking, erotic dancing and sexual indulgences were commonplace.

B. The Seduction

We saw in the scriptures that part of the entertainment for the evening was having Herodias' daughter dance. According to Josephus, her name was Salome and she was Phillip and Herodias' daughter. So Salome was Herod Antipas' step-daughter and a pawn in Herodias' hand to fan into flame the lust of Herod's heart. Verse 6 says her dance "pleased" Herod, which was nothing more than a euphemism for saying she sexually aroused him. She turned him on and the drunken and foolish king rashly promised to give her whatever she wanted. In Mark's account, he included up to half his kingdom. This was the lynchpin that Herodias had been waiting for. Suddenly, after a sidebar meeting with her mother, Salome said she wanted not half the kingdom, but instead she wanted the head of John the Baptist. She said, "Bring it to me on a platter!"

C. The Shame

Now the purpose and plan of this entire heinous plot becomes crystallized as Herod, drunk and disoriented, makes this outrageous offer to Salome. We later read that Herod was grieved about it, but he had made this pledge in front of all the guests at the party and as you remember in the Ancient Near East, a promise made with an oath was sacred and binding. Plus, he had to save face with his peers, the political and military dignitaries, who were partying with him. So the shameful and seductive scheme was accomplished. Quickly and coldly John was taken to the chopping block where he was decapitated. Now, to mock God's prophet, his head was placed on a platter, given to Salome, who in turn gave it to Herodias.

History tells us that this evil wickedness was in the genetics of Herodias, because her ancestor named Alexander Junius once held a feast in which he crucified 800 rebels simply for the entertainment of his guests. So perhaps her corrupt and carnal nature was generational. That, my friend, is no excuse! Regardless of our background or "bend", regardless of our family or failures, we all stand personally responsible before God for our actions. We live in a day when no one wants to take responsibility for their behavior. In our psychoanalytical culture, we want to try to analyze and didactically figure out why people do what they do, as if to place the blame elsewhere. Thus the question becomes was there something in our past that traumatized us or caused us to act this way? The truth is, in the 21st century, all of us are scarred from something; sexual molestation, an alcoholic dad, a broken family, a crazed uncle or just getting chosen last in a spelling bee. If we are looking for excuses we can definitely find them.

Here is what I am telling you; nothing we shamefully go through exempts us from personal responsibility but people want to place blame. I have heard this excuse so many times "I'm not interested in church because when I was growing up my parents made me go to church every time the doors were open and I'm tired of having church crammed down my throat." All I can say is, God bless your parents! They loved you enough to take you to church! It's just unfortunate that you didn't "get it" and now you're blaming them for your carnal condition.

Today, I wonder, would you lay all the excuses aside and take responsibility for your behavior? Some of you grew up with a lot and some of you grew up with nothing. For some of you things have always come easy, while for many of you life has always been difficult. All I'm saying is this, Jesus is the resolve for everyone ….regardless. But until we quit blaming others and take responsibility, we'll never discover that Jesus is enough. Jesus says come unto me all of you, every one of you. In Me you can find rest and in Me you can have life. But as Jesus declared, still, they would not come to Me that they might have life.

III. THE CONCURRING MOURNING

Then his disciples came, removed the corpse, buried it, and went and reported to Jesus. When Jesus heard about it, He withdrew from there by boat to a remote place to be alone. When the crowds heard this, they followed him on foot from the towns. As He stepped ashore, he saw a huge crowd, felt compassion for them, and healed their sick. (Matthew 14:12–14)

This despicable deed has now been done and Herodias has conspired, manipulated and accomplished her evil desire to kill John the Baptist. It seems those who are closest to this great prophet, Jesus' apostles, are notified. What we all dread and is always painful for all of us is taking those we love to their final resting place. With all my serious health issues I've had over this year, my wife, Mary, recently asked me, "Steve, if something happens to you, where do you want to be buried?" I said, "Lightning Ridge Cemetery in rural southern Oklahoma." She said, "Why there? That's over 7 hours away and we don't have any family down there anymore. It seems so out of the way." To which I said, "I know. But on the day of my funeral I want to ruin your WHOLE day! I don't want you going to the mall or getting on e-Harmony until at least the next day!" But for the followers of John the Baptist it was a solemn day in Jerusalem.

A. His Burial

So the disciples now have the unpleasant task of taking John's decapitated body to a tomb for burial. Tradition says that the body was buried at Sebaste in the West Bank. But Herodias, in her pompous and sacrilege, took the head of John and buried it in a dung heap in the Valley of Hinnom. Later it was said of Joanna; she secretly retrieved John's head and buried it on the Mount of Olives.

It's hard to imagine how devastated these disciples were, because John was their hero. He was the great, godly, gifted model in their faith and this was his undeserving destiny. Burying John was only a part of the dreaded responsibility these disciples had. They too had to go tell Jesus what had happened to John. You know, one of the things that I've dreaded more than any other assignment as a minister, is to have to go to a parent or family and tell them of a tragedy regarding their son or daughter or other family member. I love being the bearer of good news. But how woeful is the task of telling anyone that the one they care about and love is gone. That was the task given to Jesus' disciples.

B. His Brokenness

Then word came to Jesus about John's death, He responded like any of us would. He simply wants to be left alone which is understandable. The person He most respected and admired, of whom He earlier declared was the greatest man ever born of woman, was now gone. Just like He would later grieve at the tomb of Lazarus, His grief overcomes Him here. He retreated to a lonely place. As surely as Jesus grieved over John's death, He knew His day of destiny was soon coming as well when He would face the agony of Calvary, not only suffering the pain of crucifixion, but bearing the sin debt for the entire world upon His shoulders. John had declared of Jesus in John 3:30, "He must increase but I must decrease." John now at the tender age of 33, was gone and Jesus grieved and mourned over the death of His close comrade and His courageous cousin. The humanity of our Savior is never more evident than in seeing Him grieve.

This tragic and transcendent event was masterminded by a loser named Herodias and she now lives in infamy for cutting short the life of this mighty prophet of God. Honestly, every one of us is writing a legacy of our lives; whether we will be winners or losers. Really the only arena that ultimately matters is with our personal faith and my promise to you is this; if you will give your heart, your life, your all to Jesus Christ, then all the mistakes, sins and shame and all your guilt can be taken away. "For Christ also suffered for sins once for all, the righteous for the unrighteous, that he might bring you to God, after being put to death in the fleshly realm but made alive in the spiritual realm" (I Peter 3:18).

Chapter Ten

A Family Feud

II Samuel 13:1–20

I. A SEXUAL SCANDAL
- A. The Passion
- B. The Persuasion
- C. The Plot

II. A SPITEFUL SCORN
- A. The Hatefulness
- B. The Hurtfulness
- C. The Hesitation

III. A SORDID SCHEME
- A. The Conspiracy
- B. The Chaos
- C. The Commiseration

In 1976, Mark Goodson and Bill Todman produced their new television game show entitled Family Feud. It's a contest of two competing families responding to questions that had been posed to 100 people. The object of the game is to guess the most popular answers. As you remember, Richard Dawson hosted the show for 10 years and now the show is still on syndication. I still watch it occasionally.

As we look at our text from II Samuel 13, you will notice there is a family feud going on all right but it is no mere game show. It is a family feud in the house of King David. We have been on a quest to find a variety of losers in the Bible and indeed we find one now and he's in the royal family of Israel. His name is Amnon.

Amnon was the firstborn son of David. This son, the eldest of David's children, turned out to be a colossal disappointment. His foolish behavior would cost him his life and bring great grief to his father David. Children, like no other people in our lives, have the potential to make us ecstatic, proud and euphoric or, conversely, when they disobey, ignore our values and rebel against our authority, they can break our hearts and destroy our lives. As I often say, "no parent is ever any happier than their unhappiest child." That being true, King David can only be assessed as one miserable and melancholy Father. So let's consider the audacity of a son named Amnon.

I. A SEXUAL SCANDAL

Some time passed. David's son Absalom had a beautiful sister named Tamar, and David's son Amnon was infatuated with her. Amnon was frustrated to the point of making himself sick over his sister Tamar because she was a virgin, but it seemed impossible to do anything to her. Amnon had a friend named Jonadab, a son of David's brother Shimeah. Jonadab was a very shrewd man, and he asked Amnon, "Why are you, the king's son, so miserable every morning? Won't you tell me?" Amnon replied, "I'm in love with Tamar, my brother Absalom's sister." Jonadab said to him, "Lie down on your bed and pretend you're sick. When your father comes to see you, say to him, "Please let my sister Tamar come and give me something to eat. Let her prepare food in my presence so I can watch and eat from her hand." So Amnon lay down and pretended to be sick. When the king came to see him, Amnon said to him, "Please let my sister Tamar come and make a couple of cakes in my presence so I can eat from her hand." David sent word to Tamar at the palace: "Please go to your brother Amnon's house and prepare a meal for him." Then Tamar went to his house while Amnon was lying down. She took dough, kneaded it, made cakes in his presence, and baked them. She brought the pan and set it down in front of him, but he refused to eat. Amnon said, "Everyone leave me!" And everyone left him. "Bring the meal to the bedroom," Amnon told Tamar, "so I can eat from your hand." Tamar took the cakes she had made and went to her brother Amnon's bedroom. When she brought them to him to eat, he grabbed her and said, "Come sleep with me, my sister!" "Don't, my brother!" she cried. "Don't humiliate me, for such a thing should never be done in Israel. Don't do this horrible thing! Where could I ever go with my disgrace? And you—you would be like one of the immoral men in Israel! Please, speak to the king, for he won't keep me from you." But he refused to listen to her, and because he was stronger than she was, he raped her. (II Samuel 13: 1–14)

In chapter 13 we are introduced to three of David's children. Since David had eight wives, it's not surprising he had 14 children. However, the only girl David had is mentioned here and her name is Tamar. Absalom and Tamar had the same mother, whose name was Maacah. She was undoubtedly a beautiful woman because both Absalom and Tamar are said to be strikingly beautiful people. Amnon was Tamar's half-brother and he had a crush on his sister. He had, in fact, become infatuated with her.

A. The Passion

Amnon's infatuation became an obsession. He's now making himself sick over the fact that Tamar is off limits to him. Tamar was a lady of virtue. She had remained chaste and pure. She was an early subscriber to the True Love Waits vow. Actually, The Torah required unmarried women to retain their virginity. But Amnon, like a sexual predator, is making himself sick over his inability to have sex with this beautiful young lady. Amnon's unbridled passion is simmering within his lustful heart.

The problem we deal with today is that the internet and accessibility of pornography is readily available to feed anyone and everyone's sexual obsession. Since temperance and self control is a battle for every man, if you feed your sexually obsessed mind with images and pictures and opportunities even the strongest of men will soon bite the dust. The list of victims is endless and we have men in our church today who would say from their own experience,

"Stay away. Don't go there. It will wreck your life." It is the battle that every man faces.

B. The Persuasion

Amnon's cousin, Jonadab, was also his close friend. The text says of Jonadab that he was shrewd. He is the only person in the Bible described in this manner with the Hebrew word "hakam". The word could be rendered wise, but Jonadab's wisdom and shrewdness was carnal, crass, and immoral and he had a great influence over Amnon.

Isn't that the way it works? Somebody always comes along and takes us by the hand and leads us down the path to destruction and ruin. That's why parents are so concerned about who their kids hang around with. Peer influence is critical, not just in Jr. High but as adults as well. I wonder with you, do the people you hang around with cause you to want to be better? Are they challenging you to good and Godly things or do they always have a persuasive idea that will lead you to shameful things? So it was with Amnon's cousin and now we see Jonadab's idea.

C. The Plot

Jonadab's plot begins with having Amnon pretend to be ill and David, being a good dad, comes to check on his ailing son. Amnon tells him, I know what will make me feel better. Send my beautiful sister in here and let me eat from her hand. Then I'll be better. Whatever! You don't think Amnon snickered under his breath, do you? All I can say is David was more naïve than I would have been. If this would have been one of my two sons, this plot would have imploded right there! But David sends Tamar over and being the proper and thoughtful daughter she was, she rushes over to Amnon's residence. He clears the room from the rest of the household servants so he can be alone with her. She resists, she pleads with him, but Amnon is far beyond being rational and he has thrown his religious convictions out the door and he rapes her. Christian psychologist, Dr. Norman Wright said: "The closer a man gets to sexual immorality, the more unreal God becomes."[18] Tamar is appealing to his honor and dignity but Amnon didn't care about that, he didn't care about God's law, God's will or Tamar's plea. He wanted to have sex with her and that's all that mattered. Now the fantasy of all that Amnon had lewdly and lustfully imagined was over and how much satisfaction did it bring? NONE! And that's the way sexual sin will always treat you. It promises so much, but delivers so little.

Let's look at Amnon's response.

II. A SPITEFUL SCORN

Amnon's response is a bit outrageous. He's made himself sick looking and lusting after Tamar and now that he has fulfilled his fantasy, he can't stand her.

A. The Hatefulness

Amnon, because of shame, guilt and an unfulfilled soul sends her away like a cheap prostitute. The girl he was willing to die for ten minutes earlier, he now disdains and deplores. So he calls a personal servant to throw her out and bolt the door behind her.

B. The Hurtfulness

We're told that Tamar was wearing a richly adorned robe. The Holman Christian Standard Bible says a long-sleeved robe while the King James Version says a robe of many colors. It is actually the same Hebrew word used to describe Joseph's coat in Genesis 37. This was something David had given to her as an encouragement and reward for staying sexually pure. But now all of her dreams and desires came crashing down and she, in a fit of grief and mourning, tears her robe and puts ashes on her head. This foolish and forceful man has destroyed her dreams and aspirations for a future husband and she now becomes a castaway living in the house of her brother Absalom.

C. The Hesitation

David found out about this fiasco and now he's furious. Some may wonder why he didn't confront Amnon about his behavior. We can only speculate, but Amnon being fully aware of David's disgraceful behavior with Bathsheba, surely silenced the King about Amnon's escapade. Not only does David not deal with Amnon, neither does Absalom, Tamar's brother, even though this is where she has taken up residence. The text says Absalom sat silent for two years. Rest assured Absalom has been developing a plan; a master minded plot to seek revenge on his half brother, the sexual predator, Amnon. There was a day of reckoning coming. It seems sometimes we think we've gotten by with our deceit or our sinful actions only to discover we are about to harvest the consequences. Robert Lewis Stephenson said "one day we're all going to sit down to a table of consequences."[19]

In December 2009, Michael Burke was found in Veracruz, Mexico after years of being pursued by local authorities in Pennsylvania. You see, after pleading guilty back in 2004 to rape and sexual assault of a minor, he posted $100,000 bail and left the country. Michael had changed identity and thought he'd found refuge and asylum south of the border. But after five years of living shrouded in anonymity, he was found after Interpol issued an International Red Notice and Mexican authorities caught him and extradited him back to face incarceration in Pennsylvania. This proves my point that judgment may be delayed but it will not be dismissed.

Some of you reading this are living in constant fear of being found out; of someone turning states evidence against you; of having what you're doing in darkness being brought to the light. My appeal to you is to get up and out of your sin. Get things right in your life with God and with others. Ask God for mercy and forgiveness. He will not turn you away. James 2:13 says, "…mercy triumphs over judgment".

III. A SORDID SCHEME

After two years elapsed Absalom invited David and the servants to come down to Baal Hazor to the sheep shearing celebration some fourteen miles north of Jerusalem. When David refused Absalom said, "Well, since you're not going how about sending Amnon?" David suspiciously asked Absalom why he wanted Amnon to go. But Absalom, who would later prove how persuasive he could be by rallying support to take over the throne from his dad, artfully rebuffs David's reluctance and Amnon makes the trip along with the rest of David's sons as well.

A. The Conspiracy

Suddenly the narrative has moved from Jerusalem to the site of a celebration in Baal Hazor where Absalom instructs his servants to attack Amnon when he gets tipsy from the alcohol he is drinking. Here is what I notice once again, as it has been with this growing list of losers, alcohol is prevalent. This time it is the catalyst for Absalom's servants to take action. They are reluctant but upon Absalom's insistence they move forward and execute Amnon. Ironically, just as Amnon had manipulated David into getting Tamar into his chambers, now Absalom has manipulated David to get Amnon into his demise. We read that as soon as Amnon is carried out the rest of the brothers flee on their mules.

B. The Chaos

The other sons of David depart in a fury going in every direction and leaving a cloud of dust. In verse 30 we read that the word that somehow gets to David is that all his sons are dead; that Absalom has killed them all. As so often is the case when something tragic occurs and people begin to report it, it gets exaggerated and embellished and often takes on a life of its own. You can only imagine the chaos at the palace. The king, believing all of his boys are dead rips his clothes as do all of the servants. They've fallen down on the ground in exasperation and outrage. Then Jonadab, Amnon's shrewd buddy, showed up and told what really had happened. It's only Amnon who has been massacred. Then he told; David that Absalom had been planning this since Amnon disgraced Tamar. The rest of the brothers showed up confirming Jonadab's story which brings me to the third part of this conspiracy.

C. The Commiseration

When the rest of the brothers arrive, they enter weeping loudly and in unison. King David and all the attending servants are weeping too. In a chorus of sorrow the palace halls reverberate with heartache and grief. Absalom takes refuge in Goshen for three long years as he hid out from the outpouring of sorrow in Jerusalem.

What a picture, with Amnon, of the implications of sin and where it can take a person. I notice there are some curious parallels between the sin of Amnon and the sin of his father David with Bathsheba.

- First, both committed sexual sin outside of marriage with beautiful women
- Both of these encounters took place in the privacy of their own residence
- Both women experienced great grief because of the men's actions
- And ultimately both sins brought about the death of David's sons; first with the baby born to Bathsheba and now to David's son Amnon

Remember the prophet Nathan said to David after his adulterous sin with Bathsheba in the preceding chapter, "The sword will never leave your house" (II Samuel 12:10). Once again, sin has its way and the wages remain the same; death. Amnon was a loser. He lost his head and raped his sister. In turn, it cost him his life, just as the Apostle Paul wrote in Romans 6:33, "For the wages of sin is death."

Here are three lessons we can learn from the loser Amnon:

1. **Sexual sin is a great temptation.**

Amnon is no guiltier than some of you. You've been drawn away by your own lust and this lust has given birth to sin. When your sin is fully grown it will give birth to death. The Bible warns time and time again about the danger of adultery and fornication and how when one gives into sexual temptation he sins against his own body (see I Cor. 6:18).

2. Sexual sin never satisfies.

It didn't with Amnon and it won't in your life. Sexual predators are repeat offenders. Those hooked on pornography auger deeper and deeper into more seedy and more explicit material.

3. The implication of our sinful action will always be costly.

It ruins marriages, destroys trust, and its implications always linger.

Chapter Eleven

A Decision to Depart

II Timothy 4:9

I. THE ABANDONMENT

A. His Loneliness
B. His Lament
C. His Loyalty

II. THE ADORATION

A. Sensuality
B. Status
C. Self-Exaltation

III. THE ADMONISHMENT

A. The Reconciliation
B. The Relief
C. The Revelation

In II Timothy we find another obscure and little known character by the name of Demas. Paul brings him up in Chapter 4, not to honor or praise him, but to inform Timothy that he has abandoned him in his imprisonment. While he had at one time been beneficial and useful to Paul in his ministry something had dramatically changed and Paul reveals the change with four carefully crafted and chosen words saying he "loved this present age." In essence, what the love of the world had to offer had seduced Demas to not only forsake the faith but also to be drawn away and abandon Paul in his time of need. Is that sorry or what? Unfortunately we've seen this kind of thing happen before. Right in the midst of a life threatening illness or great trial of life a husband leaves his wife, a friend ignores a need, our children are indifferent, and the pain of the predicament is compounded and eclipsed by that shameful and sad behavior. Certainly in Demas we've found another loser. He lost out on what is eternal and lasting because of his infatuation with that which is temporary and insignificant. I John 1:17 says, "And the world with its lust is passing away, but the one who does God's will remains forever".

In Bunyan's famous allegorical book Pilgrim's Progress he makes mention of a character named Demas. He was a deceiver who would beckon pilgrims on the road to the Celestial City to depart from the path to join him in silver mining. Bunyan was saying in his symbolism that when people get preoccupied with the love of silver, then like Demas, they never make it to their destination of the Christian life. Let's frame our story of Demas in the context of the verse.

I. THE ABANDONMENT

Make every effort to come to me soon, for Demas has deserted me, because he loved this present world. (II Timothy 4:9–10)

As the Apostle Paul concludes the last words he would ever pen here in chapter 4 of his last epistle, he is introspective and reflective as he realizes his death is imminent. Indeed he would soon be beheaded on the Ostanian Way by the evil Emperor Nero.

A. His Loneliness

I can only imagine how lonely it would have been there in that Maritime prison. His cell was dark, cold, damp and depressing. I was watching ESPN a couple of weeks ago and they were doing a documentary on Marion Jones, the Olympic champion who was stripped of her medals. She was imprisoned in Texas after lying to the Grand Jury about taking performance enhancing drugs. She mentioned that for one span of time, 49 days, she was in solitary confinement after getting into a scuffle with another inmate. Still a charming young lady, she said the loneliness and the isolation was devastating with no company, no conversation, and no camaraderie. Surely Paul knew that feeling. That's why his plea is for Timothy to come to him soon. As he thought of Demas, his one time assistant, it grieved his soul that he had departed. The verb used here of Demas implied that Demas had not merely left him on this legitimate mission but that he had departed and forsaken Paul for good. The separation was more than just distance. It was spiritual and there is grave disappointment in the pen of the Apostle.

B. His Lament

For I am already being poured out as a drink offering, (II Timothy 4:6)

Paul understood his destiny and he knew he was not long for this world. Paul used an Old Testament analogy here comparing his life to a drink offering. A drink offering was given as the final act of the entire sacrificial ceremony after the sacrifices of goats and rams. So he was saying in essence, my life is the final sacrifice I can give fo the gospel. What was true in his death had been true in his life well. He wrote, "I beseech you therefore, brethren, by the merci God, that you present your bodies a living sacrifice, holy, acce to God, which is your reasonable service. And do not be co to this world, but be transformed by the renewing of your you may prove what is that good and acceptable and pe God" (Romans 12:1–2, NKJV).

C. His Loyalty

I have fought the good fight, I have finished th faith. There is reserved for me in the future the which the Lord, the righteous Judge, will give only to me, but to all those who have loved Hi 4:7–8)

Here Paul speaks reflectively on what h fight and the race were sports metaphors th of Paul. But this competition was more

Isthmian Games of Corinth. This was the grand fight, the ultimate race and his life had been consumed in this spiritual battle. The opposition had been real. He had battled the principalities and powers of spiritual wickedness in high places. He had battled Jewish vices and pagan practices. He had battled fanaticism, fornication, legalism and licentiousness. But now he could say with confidence, "while I've battled and fought throughout the years, I know this; there is a destiny and there is a reward that awaits me. But it's not exclusive to me but to everyone who longs to see Jesus."

Paul mentioned a crown here (literally a victor's laurel wreath), a stephanos, which would be awarded in a sporting competition to the winner. We might better understand this, as on the day we stand before God as believers in Jesus Christ, we will be given a crown that is the righteousness we need and must attain to get us to glory. II Corinthians 5:21 says, "He made the One who did not know sin to be sin for us, so that we might become the righteousness of God in Him." Our salvation and our justification are only possible through faith in Jesus Christ, the one who justifies the ungodly. Paul is saying, "I believe and I will receive all that God has waiting for me, a wreath of righteousness for my faith."

Do you understand? Your salvation is not about what you've done, but about what Jesus has done for you. It's not about church membership, baptism, catechism or confirmation, but it is about faith and that's why Paul declared, "I've kept the faith".

Now we are going to move from our focus on the Apostle Paul to our designated loser of the day, Demas.

. THE ADORATION

This is not the first mention in the Bible of Demas, this defector
e faith. Paul had mentioned him in a positive sense in Colossians
l in Philemon as a fellow worker. But now Paul says the man
nce was with me has now deserted me and it's because he has
n love with the world. In essence, the present treasures and
s of what this world has to offer had seduced him. They
yn him away from the faith and caused him to defect and
the truth of the gospel and Paul, his mentor and friend.

That's what can happen to any of us who do not guard our hearts. John put out a clear and clarion warning about this temptation, "Do not love the world or the things in the world. If anyone loves the world, the love of the Father is not in him. For all that is in the world—the lust of the flesh, the lust of the eyes, and the pride of life—is not of the Father but is of the world" (I John 2:15–16, NKJV).

This love for the present age is seductive in many facets but the following three things are chief culprits of this carnality.

A. Sensuality

Paul writes that Demas has now gone to Thessalonica. Thessalonica was the strategic capitol city of the Roman province of Macedonia. It was a large seaport city of 200,000 people. While it was a hub of pagan worship and commerce it wasn't what lined the streets that lured Demas there. No, it was what was below the streets. There was a system of underground brothels that were unrivaled in the ancient world where every carnal pleasure and perversion could be pursued and purchased. Once again, the battle that rages in the heart of every man is surely Demas' demise. This attraction is the lust of the flesh that John warns us of. It's been rather obvious in our series how often sexual sins play a part in the lives of these we've labeled as losers. We saw it with Herodias, with Jezebel, and with Amnon. This alluring lust was a battle for Demas. That's why the Bible tells us to abstain from the fleshly lusts, for they war against your soul. The Achilles heel for many is the lust of the flesh, but there is another warning that can cripple and corrupt and that is the lust of the eyes.

B. Status

While the lust of the flesh has to do with "doing" the temptation of the lust of the eyes has to do with "having". It's the pursuit and love of having the trappings, the outward appearance that indicates "we've arrived". We sometimes forget our eyes have an appetite. Have you ever heard anyone say "feast your eyes upon that!"?

Back in Biblical days the Romans and Greeks lived for entertainment and activities that excited the eyes, not unlike today. If you became a believer, in the first century, you instantly lost all status. Believers were seen as unsophisticated, ignorant and out of touch. The Apostle Paul echoed that truth as he wrote to the believers in Corinth, telling them that not many were powerful or of noble birth. Not many were wise or even strong. They were insignificant and despised in the world. But God has chosen the lowly and the unknown, those viewed as nothing by culture and society, so that no one can boast except in Jesus.

One of the earliest symbols associated with Christianity was discovered in the 2nd century near Palestine. It was a piece of graffiti and on it was drawn a donkey's head on a crucifix. The symbolism is obvious. Christians were viewed as foolish, lowly and without esteem. Anyone who worshiped Christ was seen as ignorant and foolish. Perhaps Demas was tired of being perceived by his Roman colleagues as a non-persona. He wanted status. He wanted stuff, and this stringent, selfless, sacrificial Christianity had spoiled all of that. He wanted to be a man of means.

Fast forward to the 21st century, Johnson County, Kansas, and we find ourselves conflicted about this very thing. We want nice things. We like having all the stuff and honestly when we start down this precarious path there seems to be no cure. The more we acquire the more we want; the more we get the less we're satisfied. All too often we don't own the stuff; the stuff owns us.

Maybe Demas personified what Paul wrote in I Timothy 6:10, "For the love of money is a root of all kinds of evil, and by craving it, some have wandered away from the faith and pierced themselves with many pains." I will tell you, if Demas loved the world, you can be sure he was drawn away by sensuality. But that was not his only reason for defection. It was the lust of his eyes, a yearning for status, for the love of money. Proverbs 27:20 says, "Hell and destruction are never full, so the eyes of a man are never satisfied" (NKJV). Be sure of this, if our status or our security rests upon what we own rather than who owns us, we very well will go the way of Demas. But there is another concern that duped Demas.

C. Self Exaltation

This is what the Apostle John called the "pride of life". So, the first, warning is relative to "doing", the second warning is relative to "having", but this last concern is relative to "being". It's an attitude; a disposition. It's a characteristic that makes us unusable and unacceptable in God's sight because he resists the proud. Jesus put out the forthright plea about being His disciple in Luke 9:23, "If anyone wants to come with Me, he must deny himself, take up his cross daily, and follow Me."

Demas got mesmerized by the world with its sensuality, its status symbols and his own ego. That's the altar that the world bows down to: money, sex, and power (the unholy trinity). Surely that's why Jesus told us you can't serve two masters, for either you will hate the one and love the other, or else you'll be loyal to one and despise the other. You can't serve God and money. I'm afraid Demas' problems were many of our problems as well. There is a 3 headed idol in many of our lives. We give into sexual temptation. We bow down at the altar of pornography and impurity. We pursue the American dream, wanting more and more material possessions and we buy into the lie that more stuff will bring us satisfaction and joy only to discover it only robs us. All the while our love for God is choked out by the enticements that the world has to offer. The irony of this is relative to one's evaluation of what constitutes a winner because the world's assessment is its power, prestige, possessions and prominence. But when Christ comes into our lives, He turns everything radically upside down and says it's not how many servants you have, it's how many you're willing to serve. It's not about how much you can acquire, but how much you are willing to give away. It's not about externals or the trappings of materialism. That's where man makes his evaluation but not so with God. He looks on the heart. Demas decision was deadly. He forsook the precious treasure of truth and traded it in for the trinkets of the world. "For what will it profit a man if he gains the whole world, and loses his own soul?" (Mark 8:36, NKJV).

III. THE ADMONISHMENT

Now after telling of Demas' departure, Paul admonishes Timothy about a couple of other things that are needful to him. We need a proper perspective on what really is important and what we surely should be grateful for in our lives.

A. The Reconciliation

Only Luke is with me. Bring Mark with you, for he is useful to me in the ministry. I have sent Tychicus to Ephesus. When you come, bring the cloak I left in Troas with Carpus, as well as the scrolls, especially the parchments. (II Timothy 4:11–13)

Remember, Mark had deserted Paul and Barnabas on their first missionary journey and returned home. When in Acts 15 they are starting another missionary endeavor, Barnabas wants to take Mark, but Paul refuses. There was such a sharp disagreement that they parted ways and Barnabas took Mark while Paul took Silas. They left with a strained and volatile relationship. But now they had been reconciled and were not only on good terms, but Paul says I need to have Mark with me. The Bible tells us, "As much as depends on you, live peaceably with all men" (Romans 12:18, NKJV).

B. The Relief

Paul cried out to Timothy to essentially say "it is cold here in this damp, dark dungeon and I need my cloak." It was an outer garment, much like a poncho worn for protection against the rain, the cold and the elements. Paul needed it. He needed a simple wrap. Doesn't this give us a perspective of all that we have? We sleep in warm beds, feast at a banquet table. We have more clothes than we can get in our closet and Paul, after 30 years of surrendered service to the Savior, simply says, "I need my one cloak. Please bring it to me." God help us to be satisfied with little.

C. God's Revelation

Paul asked for one last thing; the books and especially the parchments. The books were papyrus rolls. The parchments were skins of sheep, goats or calves used for writing. What was contained in those books and parchments? Undoubtedly the precious and powerful Word of God. In these remaining days he wanted to read, reflect and meditate on God's Word. So while Paul had relational needs; "bring Mark to me", he also had some physical needs; "bring my cloak" and he had some spiritual needs; "bring me God's Word for it sustains me".

As Christians we should have three expressions of gratitude:

- That we might be grateful for each other; our family, friends, children, and church family...all of our relationships.
- That we might be thankful for all of God's external blessings.
- Most importantly, that we might be expressive to our God, who is the creator, sustainer and redeemer of our lives.

Chapter Twelve

The Original Loser

I Peter 5:8

I. HIS ORIGIN
   - A. His Position
   - B. His Perfection
   - C. His Perversion
   - D. His Punishment

II. HIS OPERATION
   - A. His Mission
   - B. His Motive

III. HIS OUTCOME

In the last eleven chapters we've looked at a landscape of characters; some prominent and well known, but most of the cast have been more obscure and ambiguous. However; I want to now finish out with the one I've labeled as the "original loser". While all losers have been men and women from ancient history, this one predates them all. He cannot be addressed in past tense verbiage, because he is still at work in the world today. Of course, I'm speaking of Satan. His prominence, his power and his presence permeate the pages of the Word of God. While he is only referred to seven times in the Old Testament, every book of the New Testament deals with this adversary, for he and his demonic forces are still at work leading legions of men and women into darkness and despair. John 10:10

says, "A thief comes only to steal and to kill and to destroy. I have come so that they may have life and have it in abundance". So now we will be considering a variety of Scriptures that shed some divine light on this deceiver of darkness. I've chosen I Peter 5:8-9 as the springboard for what the Bible teaches and reveals about this evil one. It says, "Be serious! Be alert! Your adversary the Devil is prowling around like a roaring lion, looking for anyone he can devour". The clear admonition from the Apostle Peter is for believers to stay alert; to be cognizant, aware and sober-minded about the activity and prominence of the devil. Indeed we're reminded throughout the Word of God that we are in a spiritual battle. "For we do not wrestle against flesh and blood, but against principalities, against powers, against the rulers of the darkness of this age, against spiritual hosts of wickedness in the heavenly places" (Ephesians 6:12, NKJV). Peter qualifies that Satan is not merely the enemy of God; he is our adversary as well. The Greek word is translated "devil" (diabolos), where we get the English word "diabolical". This loser is diabolical in every sense of the word. He commands the demonic realm and administrates this fallen worldly system. Satan is like a predator of the night that never sleeps nor slumbers. The imagery Peter uses is a roaring lion, which obviously is a picture of viciousness and savagery; one who is hungry and pursuing his prey. Just like a lion is the king of the jungle, able to destroy its vulnerable victims, so it is with Satan. D.L. Moody said, "I believe Satan exists for two reasons. First, the Bible says it's so and secondly, I've done plenty of business with him."[20] Any kind of objective evaluation of all that is transpiring before our eyes, in our culture and in our world, is proof enough that this sinister seducer is alive and at work today. Most of Satan's activity is covert and behind the scenes, but, not always. Some of you may remember the name Sean Sellars. Sean was executed in 1999 at the McAlester State Prison in McAlester, Oklahoma for the murder of a convenience store employee, Robert Bower, and his mother and step-father in Oklahoma City. It was all brought on by a satanic ritual he had succumbed to. Before moving to Kansas City, I was the pastor at First Baptist Church of Piedmont, Oklahoma. Sean had been a student in Piedmont before transferring to the Putnam City Schools. It seems that in 1984, Sean began to get obsessed with the board game Dungeons and Dragons and he confessed that he had also read Anton Laveys Satanic Bible hundreds of times between the ages of fifteen and sixteen. This obsession led him to commit these three unspeakable atrocities, using the 357 magnum that he had stolen from Jack Collier, who was in charge of maintenance at First Baptist Church of Piedmont. Sean is the only person under the age of 18 to ever be executed in this country. At his trial he confessed that he was practicing Satanism at the time of the murders and believed demonic possession led him to kill these three innocent victims. However; satanic strategies are usually not as obvious and apparent as he works all around us. We are going to look at three things concerning this original loser.

I. HIS ORIGIN

Son of man, lament for the king of Tyre and say to him: This is what the Lord God says: You were the seal of perfection, full of wisdom and perfect in beauty. You were in Eden, the garden of God. Every kind of precious stone covered you: carnelian, topaz, and diamond, beryl, onyx, and jasper, sapphire, turquoise and emerald. Your mountings and settings were crafted in gold; they were prepared on the day you were created. You were an anointed guardian cherub, for I had appointed you. You were on the holy mountain of God; you walked among the fiery stones. From the day you were created you were blameless in your ways until wickedness was found in you. Through the abundance fyour trade, you were filled with violence and you sinned. So I expelled you in disgrace from the mountain of God, and banished you, guardian cherub, from among the fiery stones. Your heart became proud because of your beauty; for the sake of your splendor you corrupted your wisdom. So I threw you down to the earth; I made you a spectacle before kings. You profaned your sanctuaries by the magnitude of your iniquities in your dishonest trade. So I made fire come from within you, and it consumed you. I reduced you to ashes on the ground in the sight of everyone watching you. All those who know you among the nations are appalled at you. You have become an object of horror and will never exist again. (Ezekiel 28:12–19)

I will ascend above the highest clouds; I will make myself like the "Most High". But you will be brought down to Sheol into the deepest regions of the Pit. Those who see you will stare at you; they will look closely at you: "Is this the man who caused the earth to tremble, who shook the kingdoms, who turned the world into a wilderness, who destroyed its cities and would not release the prisoners to return home?" (Isaiah 14:12–17)

When God created the world, we read in Genesis 1:31, "God saw all that He had made and it was very good". But when you come to Genesis 3, we find Satan in the form of a serpent, tempting Eve to sin. So when God created the heavens and the earth there was unity, harmony, love and utopia. Job wrote in Chapter 38 that the angels sang at the creation of the world. Just like a rebellion took place on earth in the heart of Adam and Eve in the Garden of Eden, so it was preceded by another rebellion and that was by Satan and his demons. It had to take place between Genesis 1:31 and Genesis 3. According to Revelation 12:4, Satan rebelled against God and took one third of the angels with him in his coup. I have listed the two proof texts above that reveal the fall of Satan. Let's look at them and see what we can learn. While contextually Isaiah writes about the king of Babylon and Ezekiel about the king of Tyre we see a dual application in these prophetic texts.

A. His Position

According to Isaiah 14 the guardian cherub was full of wisdom and beauty. In Fred Dickerson's book Angels he describes a cherub as the greatest class and highest order of celestial beings. With these descriptions, Lucifer was the greatest of the cherubs. He is twice called the guardian cherub. He was an honored angel; a messenger at God's disposal. Undoubtedly Lucifer had an exalted position in the hierarchy of angels who served Jehovah.

B. His Perfection

"You were perfect in your ways from the day you were created, till iniquity was found in you" (Ezekiel 28:15, NKJV). The name Lucifer means "shining one"; the star of the morning. He was uniquely beautiful, perfect and pure. In the Latin Vulgate he is called the "light bearer".

Understand this, since God is holy and perfect, by His very nature, He cannot be involved in the creation of anything evil. Thus, when God created the entire heavenly host, He created them as holy angels. They were perfect and created to serve God. However; all that would change.

C. His Perversion

In Ezekiel 28:15 the text says, without any explanation, that iniquity was found in him. Verse 17 explains it to us, "Your heart became proud because of your beauty; for the sake of your splendor you corrupted your wisdom". The root of the problem was a proud heart and it was because of his proud heart that God cast him down to the earth. The parallel passage in Isaiah 14:13–15 says, "You said to yourself: "I will ascend to the heavens, I will set up my throne above the stars of God. I will sit on the mount of the gods' assembly, in the remotest parts of the North. I will ascend above the highest clouds; I will make myself like the "Most High". Lucifer uses the personal pronoun "I will" five times in this passage, which also uniquely fits the description of the coming anti-Christ, portrayed in II Thessalonians as a proud rebel. First, Lucifer declares in verse 13:

1. "I will ascend into heaven".

Already having access to the very presence of God as the leading cherub, he was not saying, "I think I'll go visit God". No, Satan was saying, "I will go and I will remain". His intent was to occupy the throne of God. I will ascend…" as the chief angel, the only person left between him and God was God Himself. He was saying, "I will take over for God."

2. "I will exalt my throne above the stars of God".

In other words he was boasting, "I will usurp God's authority over the angels. I will take over as ruler of heaven and earth".

3. **"I will sit also upon the mount of the congregation, in the sides of the north".**

According to Isaiah 2:2 and Psalm 48:2, "the mount of the congregation" is the center of God's kingdom rule. So, in essence, he was saying, "I will rule in place of Messiah".

4. **"I will ascend above the heights of the clouds".**

Most commentators would say that the clouds refer to the glory of God. Lucifer wanted glory above that of God.

5. **"I will be like the Most High".**

Did you know that the "Most High" is God's title as possessor of heaven and earth? This is the very position Satan was hoping to gain.

Because of egotism, pride and arrogance Lucifer fell from his prominence in God's host of heavenly beings. Jesus gave testimony of this rebellion when He said in Luke 10:18, "I watched Satan fall from heaven like a lightning flash".

D. His Punishment

Because of his rebellion, he was exiled from the presence of God. We read in Isaiah 14, "you were expelled to the pit" and the once privileged and prominent cherub was cast down. He lost what once was his. As we later will see Satan's ultimate punishment will be fulfilled at the end of the millennial reign of Christ.

So it seems pride, egotism, a hunger for power turn an angel into a devil and Lucifer's judgment was realized. But once again we see the destructive pathway of pride. Lucifer lost sight of God's sovereignty and supremacy. I'm afraid in our self-centered, me-focused world we often are guilty of the same. We think it is all about us! Be sure of this; God sends no one away empty except those who are full of themselves.

Here's what I know; pride goes before a fall. It was true with Lucifer and it will be true in your life and in mine. This fallen one is a prototype of what we must avoid. He is the enemy. He is always sowing seeds of discord among the brethren. Be sure, these 5 "I wills" of Satan still rear their ugly head in churches today and it can become like a virus. It forms little pockets of pride, jealousy and discontentment because people want to be first and want what they prefer. Satan will use egos and self-centeredness to cripple a congregation and your life.

II. HIS OPERATION

Be serious! Be alert! Your adversary the Devil is prowling around like a roaring lion, looking for anyone he can devour. (I Peter 5:8)

In Peter's epistle he uses the imagery of a roaring lion, roaring and seeking with the objective of destroying, ripping to shreds and gulping down its victims. Understand this about Satan; he is not equal with God. Some people are confused about his authority and power. While we need to be alert and on guard against his onslaught of attacks, we always must remember he is a defeated foe. He sails a sinking ship. Our call is to live surrendered lives in obedience to our Savior, for He and only He is omnipresent, omniscient and omnipotent. Still, God's word tells us to be informed, alert and on guard.

A. His Mission

Satan has a purpose to destroy, devastate, tear you down and leave you destitute. While Satan is not omnipresent, he has with him a legion of principalities and powers; tens of millions of demons to accomplish heinous and satanic schemes. So his mission is to destroy what God engineers. Satan's legacy is everywhere you look. Every sinner and every sin points back to him. I John 3:8 says, "The one who commits sin is of the Devil, for the Devil has sinned from the beginning. The Son of God was revealed for this purpose: to destroy the Devil's works". Honestly, all of us are either growing into the image of God or into the likeness of Satan and his mission can best be understood as one who counterfeits. He distorts truth, promotes cultic and counterfeit ideologies. He advocates humanism, atheism; everything and anything that points people away from saving faith in Jesus Christ. His mission is revealed in the names that the Bible has given him:

- He is our adversary
- He is an accuser of the brethren (slanderer)
- Belial, which means worthless or ruin (see II Corinthians 6)
- Dragon, ancient serpent (see Revelation 20)
- Tempter (see Matthew 4)
- Father of lies
- God of this world, prince and power of the air

The Apostle Paul writes of this mission in II Corinthians 4:4 which says, "In their case, the god of this age has blinded the minds of the unbelievers so they cannot see the light of the gospel of the glory of Christ, who is the image of God".

B. His Motive

Satan's motive is to mislead you, to cause you to doubt God's existence, God's love, God's plan and God's preeminence. His deception is dubious. In II Corinthians 11 the Apostle Paul mentions false apostles, deceitful workers and how they were mimicking true apostles and making themselves out to be authentic. He is saying no wonder Satan himself transforms himself into an angel of light. No doubt, Satan and his forces show up in the most respectable and even reverent places and subtly worm their way in, using people, situations and relationships to destroy families, churches, kingdom work and all that God passionately desires. I'm convinced one of Satan's motives of deception is to have you deny his existence. Certainly many liberal theologians have taken the bait and denied that Satan is real. But if you believe the Bible you realize he is as Peter declares; not only real but a roaring lion.

According to James Patterson and Peter Kim in their book, The Day America Told the Truth, 82% of Americans believe in the afterlife and believe that Heaven and Hell are real places while only 55% of people believe in the existence of Satan. So, on one hand we have multitudes who deny Satan's existence and on the other extreme, we have a neo-Pentecostal group that attributes every bad habit, every misfortune, every illness and even a bad weather day to him. They believe there is a demon behind every bush. We should avoid either extreme.

God's Word is clear. We are to stay alert to his purposes and his plans but we must also remember Satan cannot do anything to usurp God's will and God's consent. Why God allows what He does is often an enigma. It is indeed a mystery. In Calvin's Commentary, he sees Satan's object and his options this way: "He eagerly and of set purpose opposes God, aiming at those things which he deems most contrary to the will of God. But as God holds him bound and fettered by the curb of his power, he executes those things only for which permission has been given him. Thus, however unwilling, obeys his Creator, being forced…to do Him service."[21] As we study the mission, the motive, and the operation of Satan, we must remember, as the Apostle John assured us in I John 4:4, "…the one who is in you is greater than the one who is in the world".

III. HIS OUTCOME

It seems no one, whether human or angelic, can escape the wages of sin. Lucifer will pay for his rebellion and the angels who went with him will as well. We read about the coming judgment in the New Testament. Just like the Bible tells us that it is appointed for every man to face judgment; so it will also be with Satan. Actually, there have been three Biblical judgments already on Satan and three more await him.

1. The first judgment was when, because of his rebellion against God, he was cast out of heaven. (see Ezekiel 28)

2. Then, secondly, after the fall of man in the Garden of Eden in Genesis 3, God pronounced judgment on the serpent.

3. The great judgment that we revel in is the one that took place on a hill called Calvary, as the Son of God was there, suspended between heaven and earth, bearing the iniquities of the world.

Jesus said, "Now is the judgment of this world; now the ruler of this world will be cast out. And I, if I am lifted up from the earth, will draw all peoples to myself" (John 12:31–32, NKJV). You see, at Calvary, the fetters of sin that had bound the heart of every man were loosed because, through the person and work of Jesus Christ, redemption, restoration, renewal and freedom were purchased. Now through faith in Him, we have victory over death, hell and Satan himself. Paul wrote, "Yet in all these things we are more than conquerors through Him who loved us. For I am persuaded that neither death nor life, nor angels nor principalities nor powers, nor things present nor things to come, nor height nor depth, nor any other created thing, shall be able to separate us from the love of God which is in Christ Jesus our Lord" (Romans 8:37–39, NKJV). If you are reading this and you have never trusted Christ, you are still on the losing side. But, if you will trust in the One who is the Overcomer, you can have eternal life.

The other judgments that await Satan are eschatological, for we read in Revelation 12 that he will be cast out in the midst of tribulation and later, in Revelation 20, that he will be confined to the abyss at the beginning of the millennium. But, ultimately, his fate takes him to be cast alive into the Lake of Fire. "The devil, who deceived them, was cast into the lake of fire and brimstone where the beast and the false prophet are. And they will be tormented day and night forever and ever" (Revelation 20:10, NKJV). It will be in that place of eternal damnation where all the losers throughout the ages will unite, but for anyone here, the hope is still in Jesus Christ, the Savior and the Victor, who has purchased for us so great a salvation.

Conclusion

I hope that reading Life's Lessons from Life's Losers has inspired you and reminded you that rebellion against God has serious consequences. What was true in biblical days is still true today. The resounding theme in every chapter is what Moses wrote back in the Pentateuch; "be sure your sins will find you out" (Numbers 32:23, KJV). Certainly it was true for every one of these characters—their iniquity was revealed and it lead these perpetrators to death and destruction.

The reason for the writing of this book is because there is hope for forgiveness to all who call upon the Lord Jesus, for He and only He is the hope of salvation. The scripture clearly states, "Neither is there salvation in any other, for there is none other name under heaven given among men, whereby we must be saved (Acts 4:12, KJV).

My prayer is that God would use this book to draw many to Himself. First, I pray that those who have never given their heart to Christ would repent and believe the gospel. I also pray that those believers who have allowed sin to make its way into their lives would come to their senses and return to their loving Heavenly Father.

Acts 3:19,
Pastor Steve Dighton

About the Author

Steve Dighton has pastored for 28 years. He has served as President of the Kansas/Nebraska convention of Southern Baptists, has been VP of the Pastor's Conference of the SBC, and has taught at Midwestern Baptist Theological Seminary. He has a love for God, for people and a passion to see those who are without Christ come to faith in Him. In this first book, Life's Lessons from Life's Losers, he puts out the warning, that without Christ everyone will ultimately be a loser. The Bible is full of big losers, both men and women, who choose to ignore their creator and redeemer and live hopelessly in unbelief. Steve is a gifted pastor who not only preaches the Word of God unashamedly but also loves and cares for the people of God. He lives with his wife, Mary, in Lenexa, Kansas. He has two sons and four grandchildren.

End Notes

1 Harold L. Willmington, Willmington's Guide to the Bible (Wheaton, IL: Tyndale House, 1982)

2 www.quotationspage.com/quote/28723.html

3 Arthur T. Pierson, Many Infallible Proofs (Chicago, IL: F.H. Revell, 1886)

4 "Antinomy." Merriam–Webster's Online Dictionary and Thesaurus. 2011. Web

5 Boyd Bailey, Wisdom Hunters, http://www.wisdomhunters.com

6 John R.W. Stott, The Cross of Christ (Downers Grove, IL: InterVarsity Press, 2006)

7 Charles R. Swindoll, Swindoll's Ultimate Book of Illustrations and Quotes (Nashville, TN: Thomas Nelson, Inc., 1998)

8 John H. Yates, "Faith is the Victory", 1891, Baptist Hymnal #413 (Convention Press, 1991)

9 John Piper, Desiring God (Colorado Springs, CO: Multnomah Books, 2003)

10 "Loser." Merriam–Webster Online Dictionary and Thesaurus. 2011. Web

11 Oscar Wilde, Oscar Wilde's Wit and Wisdom (Mineola, NY: Dover Publications, 1998)

12 www.friendsofVanceHavner.org/quotes.html

13 www.goodreads.com/quotes/show/233515.html

14 Dr. Herbert Lockyer R.S.L., All The Women of the Bible (Grand Rapid, MI: Zondervan Publishing House)

15 www.newsforchristians.com Classic Sermon Library, "Payday Someday" by R.G. Lee
16 John MacArthur, Jr., The MacArthur New Testament Commentary Matthew 8–15 (Chicago, IL: MoodyPress, 1989)
17 Baptists Today, June 29, 1993, 23.
18 Dr. H. Norman Wright, One Marriage U nder God (Colorado Springs, CO: Multnomah Publishers, Inc., 2005)
19 www.quotationsbook.com/quote/8149.html
20 Albert M. Wells, Jr., Inspiring Quotations (Nashville, TN: Thomas Nelson, Inc., 1988)
21 John Calvin, Institutes of the Christian Religion Vol. 1 (London: Forgotten Books, 2007)